SURELY THERE IS A FUTURE

INTERNATIONAL THEOLOGICAL COMMENTARY

Fredrick Carlson Holmgren and George A. F. Knight
General Editors

Volumes now available

SURELY THERE IS A FUTURE

A Commentary on the Book of

Ruth

E. JOHN HAMLIN

WM. B. EERDMANS PUBLISHING CO., GRAND RAPIDS

THE HANDSEL PRESS LTD, EDINBURGH

© 1996 Wm. B. Eerdmans Publishing Company
First published 1996 by Wm. B. Eerdmans Publishing Company,
255 Jefferson Ave. S.E., Grand Rapids, Michigan 49503
and
The Handsel Press Limited
The Stables, Carberry EH21 8PY, Scotland

00 99 98 97 96   7 6 5 4 3 2 1

Library of Congress Cataloging-in-Publication Data

Hamlin, E. John.
Surely there is a future: a commentary on the book of Ruth /
E. John Hamlin.
p.   cm. — (International theological commentary)
Includes bibliographical references.
ISBN 0-8028-4150-3 (paper: alk. paper)
1. Bible. O.T. Ruth — Commentaries. I. Title. II. Series.
BS1315.3.H36 1996
222'.3507 — dc20   95-44352
                                              CIP

Handsel Press ISBN 1-871828-30-9

CONTENTS

ABBREVIATIONS

JB	Jerusalem Bible
KJV	King James (or Authorized) Version
LXX	Septuagint
NAB	New American Bible
NEB	New English Bible
NIV	New International Version
NJPS	New Jewish Publication Society version
NRSV	New Revised Standard Version
RSV	Revised Standard Version
REB	Revised English Bible
TEV	Today's English Version

EDITORS' PREFACE

The Old Testament alive in the Church: this is the goal of the *International Theological Commentary*. Arising out of changing, unsettled times, this Scripture speaks with an authentic voice to our own troubled world. It witnesses to God's ongoing purpose and to God's caring presence in the universe without ignoring those experiences of life that cause one to question God's existence and love. This commentary series is written by front-rank scholars who treasure the life of faith.

Addressed to ministers and Christian educators, the *International Theological Commentary* moves beyond the usual critical-historical approach to the Bible and offers a *theological* interpretation of the Hebrew text. Thus, engaging larger textual units of the biblical writings, the authors of these volumes assist the reader in the appreciation of the theology underlying the text as well as its place in the thought of the Hebrew Scriptures. But more, since the Bible is the book of the believing community, its text has acquired ever more meaning through an ongoing interpretation. This growth of interpretation may be found both within the Bible itself and in the continuing scholarship of the Church.

Contributors to the *International Theological Commentary* are Christians — persons who affirm the witness of the New Testament concerning Jesus Christ. For Christians, the Bible is *one* Scripture containing the Old and New Testaments. For this reason, a commentary on the Old Testament may not ignore the second part of the canon, namely, the New Testament.

Since its beginning, the Church has recognized a special relationship between the two Testaments. But the precise character of this bond has been difficult to define. Thousands of books and

vii

articles have discussed the issue. The diversity of views represented in these publications makes us aware that the Church is not of one mind in expressing the "how" of this relationship. The authors of this commentary share a developing consensus that any serious explanation of the Old Testament's relationship to the New will uphold the integrity of the Old Testament. Even though Christianity is rooted in the soil of the Hebrew Scriptures, the biblical interpreter must take care lest he or she "christianize" these Scriptures.

Authors writing in this commentary will, no doubt, hold varied views concerning *how* the Old Testament relates to the New. No attempt has been made to dictate one viewpoint in this matter. With the whole Church, we are convinced that the relationship between the two Testaments is real and substantial. But we recognize also the diversity of opinions among Christian scholars when they attempt to articulate fully the nature of this relationship.

In addition to the Christian Church, there exists another people for whom the Old Testament is important, namely, the Jewish community. Both Jews and Christians claim the Hebrew Bible as Scripture. Jews believe that the basic teachings of this Scripture point toward, and are developed by, the Talmud, which assumed its present form about 500 C.E. On the other hand, Christians hold that the Old Testament finds its fulfillment in the New Testament. The Hebrew Bible, therefore, belongs to both the Church and the Synagogue.

Recent studies have demonstrated how profoundly early Christianity reflects a Jewish character. This fact is not surprising because the Christian movement arose out of the context of first-century Judaism. Further, Jesus himself was Jewish, as were the first Christians. It is to be expected, therefore, that Jewish and Christian interpretations of the Hebrew Bible will reveal similarities *and* disparities. Such is the case. The authors of the *International Theological Commentary* will refer to the various Jewish traditions that they consider important for an appreciation of the Old Testament text. Such references will enrich our understanding of certain biblical passages and, as an extra gift, offer us insight into the relationship of Judaism to early Christianity.

An important second aspect of the present series is its *international* character. In the past, Western church leaders were considered to be *the* leaders of the Church — at least by those living in the West! The theology and biblical exegesis done by these scholars dominated the thinking of the Church. Most commentaries were produced in the Western world and reflected the lifestyle, needs, and thoughts of its civilization. But the Christian Church is a worldwide community. People who belong to this universal Church reflect differing thoughts, needs, and lifestyles.

Today the fastest growing churches in the world are to be found, not in the West, but in Africa, Indonesia, South America, Korea, Taiwan, and elsewhere. By the end of this century, Christians in these areas will outnumber those who live in the West. In our age, especially, a commentary on the Bible must transcend the parochialism of Western civilization and be sensitive to issues that are the special problems of persons who live outside of the "Christian" West, issues such as race relations, personal survival and fulfillment, liberation, revolution, famine, tyranny, disease, war, the poor, and religion and state. Inspired of God, the authors of the Old Testament knew what life is like on the edge of existence. They addressed themselves to everyday people who often faced more than everyday problems. Refusing to limit God to the "spiritual," they portrayed God as one who heard and knew the cries of people in pain (see Exod. 3:7-8). The contributors to the *International Theological Commentary* are persons who prize the writings of these biblical authors as a word of life to our world today. They read the Hebrew Scriptures in the twin contexts of ancient Israel and our modern day.

The scholars selected as contributors underscore the international aspect of the series. Representing very different geographical, ideological, and ecclesiastical backgrounds, they come from more than seventeen countries. Besides scholars from such traditional countries as England, Scotland, France, Italy, Switzerland, Canada, New Zealand, Australia, South Africa, and the United States, contributors from the following places are included: Israel, Indonesia, India, Thailand, Singapore, Taiwan, and countries of Eastern Europe. Such diversity makes for richness of thought. Christian scholars living in Buddhist, Muslim, or Socialist lands may be able to offer the World Church insights into the biblical message — insights to which the scholarship of the West could be blind.

The proclamation of the biblical message is the focal concern of the *International Theological Commentary*. Generally speaking, the authors of these commentaries value the historical-critical studies of past scholars, but they are convinced that these studies by themselves are not enough. The Bible is more than an object of critical study; it is the revelation of God. In the written Word, God has disclosed himself and his will to humankind. Our authors see themselves as servants of the Word which, when rightly received, brings *shalom* to both the individual and the community.

GEORGE A. F. KNIGHT
FREDRICK CARLSON HOLMGREN

AUTHOR'S PREFACE

What began as a single volume on Joshua, Judges, and Ruth, as originally requested by George Knight fifteen years ago, has now become three volumes, thanks to the patience and encouragement of International Theological Commentary editors Knight and Fred Holmgren. Thanks are due to those who generously gave of their time to read and comment on the manuscript: former colleagues in Thailand Kamol Aryaprateeb, Herbert Grether, and Marjorie McIlvride, good neighbors Ben Lane and Margaret Gebhart, sister-in-law Virginia Sherertz, and niece Nancy Sherertz. Throughout the writing of all three volumes, Frances Jane Cade Hamlin has been at my side, always ready to proofread, clear up grammatical points, and spur me on in times of flagging spirits, for which I express my deep appreciation and gratitude.

E. JOHN HAMLIN

xi

INTRODUCTION

The book of Ruth, set in the period of the judges, is a beautiful story of the love, covenant loyalty, and daring initiative of two impoverished widows. Together with a generous open-hearted man, they demonstrate the truth of a proverb that applies to individuals, families, communities, and nations: "Surely there is a future, and your hope will not be cut off" (Prov. 23:18). Future and hope are the will of Yahweh, whose hidden hand is at work creating opportunities and opening doors for people to respond with covenant loyalty.

There are at least four perspectives from which the reader may approach the book of Ruth: (1) as literature, (2) as history, (3) as part of the canon, and (4) as truth-telling story.

THE BOOK OF RUTH AS LITERATURE

Ruth is a beautiful, well-crafted narrative similar to those about Joseph (Gen. 37, 39–50), Jonah, and Esther. It is to be enjoyed as a prime example of the storyteller's art. We will call the story-teller the "Narrator," and agree that he or she was a literary "genius" (Edward F. Campbell, Jr., *Ruth*, 10). With this perspective in mind, this commentary will pay attention to the development of the plot, key words, and speeches by the main and secondary characters (see Campbell, *Ruth*, 10-18).

THE BOOK OF RUTH AS HISTORY

The story has a historical background. It is set in a particular historical period (Ruth 1:1) and tells about real people. However, it is not a factual historical account by an eyewitness. It is a literary work, composed long after the events described. The intended readers no longer understood customs of former times (4:7-8). David had already made a "name in Bethlehem" as Israel's greatest king (4:11, 17).

Most scholars today believe that the Narrator composed this story in the time of the Monarchy (1020-587 B.C.). Some prefer a date as early as the reign of David (1000-961) or Solomon (961-923). Others believe that the reign of Josiah (640-609) or the postexilic community in the time of Ezra and Nehemiah (464-358) provide the most plausible background for the story. In this commentary we agree with those who date it in the early Monarchy. Edward F. Campbell, Jr. (*Ruth*, 28) suggests the period between 950 (Solomon) and 700 (Hezekiah). The reign of Solomon (961-922) is perhaps most likely (see Robert L. Hubbard, *The Book of Ruth*, 46). Robert Alter has described this period as "the golden age of Hebrew narrative" (Robert Alter and Frank Kermode, *The Literary Guide to the Bible*, 30).

THE BOOK OF RUTH AS PART OF THE CANON

When the editors of the biblical canon arranged the books in order, they placed the book of Ruth in the context of all the other books of the Bible. With this canonical context in mind, we will look for connections, allusions, themes, similarities, and contrasts between the book of Ruth and other parts of Scripture. Two different canonical settings provide different perspectives from which to view the book.

Associated with the History of Israel

In the Greek OT (LXX) and the Christian canon, the book of Ruth is situated between Judges and 1-2 Samuel. The editors understood it as a part of Israel's sacred history from Abraham to the fall of Jerusalem. This setting invites a search for possible connections with the Pentateuch, Joshua, Judges, 1-2 Samuel and 1-2 Kings, Ezra and Nehemiah. Mention of Rachel, Leah, and

Tamar (Ruth 4:11-12) links the story to the traditions of the foremothers in Gen. 29–31, 38. Proximity to Joshua and Judges and 1 Samuel invites comparisons with the stories of Rahab (Josh. 2), the Levite's concubine (Judg. 19–21), and the Song of Hannah (1 Sam. 2:1-10). The story of Ruth also points forward to David, Israel's greatest king, and in its canonical context to the new Davidic king, the Messiah to come.

Associated with Israel's Annual Agricultural Cycle

The editors of the Hebrew Bible grouped the book of Ruth with the five festal scrolls *(megilloth)*, each of which were read at an annual festival: the Song of Songs at Passover, the book of Ruth at the Festival of Weeks marking the end of the wheat harvest, Lamentations on the 9th of Ab recalling the destruction of Jerusalem, Ecclesiastes at the Festival of Tabernacles or New Year, and Esther at Purim. In this canonical setting the book of Ruth is related more naturally with the annual cycle of "seedtime and harvest, cold and heat, summer and winter, day and night" (Gen. 8:22). Many parts of the books of Psalms and Proverbs resonate with the book of Ruth in this setting. Moreover, this setting links the story of Ruth with all peoples of the earth. Whether the harvest is of grain, vegetables, or fruit, the experience of harvest is universal. All peoples have their harvest festivals. In this canonical setting, the book of Ruth has a timeless, universal appeal.

THE BOOK OF RUTH AS MESSAGE

As we read the book of Ruth from the above three perspectives, we find that it is witness to God's truth in the midst of today's realities. "Story and not history," says David J. A. Clines, is "the primary mode of communication of religious truth." The story offers a world into which the reader enters and participates (*The Theme of the Pentateuch*, 102). It is the biblical text, says Walter Brueggemann, that "creates the church . . . [if the audience] will imagine itself to be the audience intended by the text" ("The Preacher, the Text, and the People," 244). We will try to assume the role of the "intended audience" as we move through the text, and will consider the message of the story further in the concluding part of this commentary.

THE REMNANT

Ruth 1:1-5

WHEN THE JUDGES RULED

Unlike stories that begin with "once upon a time in a far off land . . . ," the story of Ruth is specific as to time: the chaotic and violent period of the judges, that is, after the death of Joshua, the successor to Moses (Judg. 1:1), and before the appearance of Samuel (1 Sam. 1:20), who anointed David as the future king of Israel (1 Sam. 16:13). The force of these seven introductory words, "In the days when the judges ruled . . . ," is this: when violence against women, vengeance, idolatry, death, and disintegration were widespread as in the days of the judges, God's hidden hand was at work preparing a future for the survivor, her family, and her people, and, from a NT perspective, for all peoples of the earth.

FOCUS ON BETHLEHEM

The central importance of Bethlehem in the story of Ruth is shown by the Narrator's careful choice of words. As the story begins, the family leaves Bethlehem for Moab. Then Naomi, with Ruth by her side, returns to Bethlehem (Ruth 1:19), the home of Boaz (2:4). At the end of the story, the wishes of the people of Bethlehem are that the son to be born to Ruth the Moabite will bring fame ("a name") to Bethlehem (4:11). This in turn points to the birth of David in Bethlehem (4:17).

"Bethlehem in Judah"

The main action of the story takes place in the historical city of "Bethlehem in Judah" (Ruth 1:1, 2). Readers will note that the last two episodes of idolatry and violence in the book of Judges both begin in "Bethlehem in Judah" (Judg. 17:7, 9; 19:1, 18). Against that background, the Narrator seems to suggest that the story of Ruth, beginning and ending in "Bethlehem in Judah," marks a new era of covenant faithfulness and loyalty. Readers of the NT will also note that this exact phrase does not occur again in the OT, but that the phrase "Bethlehem of Judea" is once again the place where a new beginning is made with the birth of Jesus (Matt. 2:1, 5).

"Ephrathites from Bethlehem in Judah"

Elimelech and his family are identified as "Ephrathites from Bethlehem in Judah" (Ruth 1:2). By using this phrase at the beginning, the Narrator points to the end of the story where Ruth and Boaz will "prosper in Ephrathah" (Ruth 4:11 RSV). The significance of Ephrathah in the story of Ruth becomes clear when we note that the only other occurrence of the phrase "Ephrathites from Bethlehem in Judah" in the OT is the description of David as the "son of an Ephrathite of Bethlehem in Judah" (1 Sam. 17:12). Micah drew on this tradition when he told of a coming ruler to be born in "Bethlehem of Ephrathah" (Mic. 5:2).

Focus on Bethlehem makes the story of Ruth the beginning point of a trajectory that extends to the time when Bethlehem will be known as David's city (1 Sam. 20:6), the prophecy that Bethlehem would be the birthplace of a new David (Mic. 5:2), and on to the NT period when "the city of David called Bethlehem" was to be the birthplace of "a Savior, who is the Messiah" (Luke 2:4, 11). Popular belief was that "the Messiah is descended from David and comes from Bethlehem, the village where David lived" (John 7:42).

6

FAMINE

The words "there was a famine in the land" (Ruth 1:1) link the story of Ruth with the stories about the foremothers and forefathers. Famine also motivated Abraham and Sarah, Isaac and Rebekah, and Jacob and his family to cross borders into Egypt or the land of the Philistines in search of food (Gen. 12:10; 26:1; 41:57; 43:1). Famine also links the story of Ruth with famines in the time of David (2 Sam. 21:1), Elijah (1 Kgs. 18:2), Elisha (2 Kgs. 6:25), Jeremiah (Jer. 16:4), and Zedekiah (2 Kgs. 25:3; cf. Lam. 5:10; Ezek. 7:15).

The Hebrew word translated "famine" can also be translated as "hunger," which causes not only terrible craving for food (Isa. 32:6; cf. Lam. 2:19-20), but also crime, deep anguish, social breakdown (Isa. 8:21-22), and the degradation of slavery (1 Sam. 2:5). Famine makes Elimelech and his family kin to hungry people "in every country . . . throughout the world" (Gen. 41:54, 57) in every age.

The Narrator does not tell us anything about the cause of the famine that begins the book of Ruth. Was it the result of failure of rainfall, the chaos of the "days when the judges ruled," warfare, selfishness, or a struggle for power? Were its effects made worse by the failure of people to open their hands to the poor (cf. Deut. 15:11)? Whatever the reason, the severity of the famine caused Naomi and her family to move to "the country of Moab." Finally, however, the story of Ruth leads on to a plentiful harvest in the "field of Judah." This major theme of the story, from famine to plenty, from emptiness to fullness, recurs throughout the Bible:

> For he satisfies the thirsty,
> and the hungry he fills with good things.
> (Ps. 107:9; cf. 1 Sam. 2:5; Luke 1:53)

RISKY SOJOURN IN MOAB

In the days of the judges, Moab was an independent kingdom east of the Dead Sea, extending from the Brook Zered, not far from the southern end of the Dead Sea, to a point a few kilometers

7

north of the sea. Running north and south along the 40 km. (25 mi.) wide territory was a narrow strip of well-watered land that produced fine crops of grain. We may think of Elimelech and his family crossing the Jordan near Jericho, making the steep ascent to the Plains of Moab, and turning south along the King's Highway that was a major communication route between Egypt and Damascus.

"The Country of Moab"

Further insight into the Narrator's design will come from an examination of two uses of one Hebrew word. The phrase "the country (Heb. *sadeh*) of Moab" occurs seven times (Ruth 1:1, 2, 6 [twice], 22; 2:6; 4:3). It was the place *to which* the family went to live for ten years as temporary residents (note the word "sojourn," 1:1 RSV), and *from which* Ruth and Naomi went (1:6) on their way back to "the land of Judah" (1:7).

"The Field of Judah"

By a clever wordplay, the Narrator has used the same Hebrew word *(sadeh)* seven times to refer to the "field" of Judah, specifically Boaz's "field" or "another field" (2:2, 3 [twice], 8, 9, 17, 22), and twice to refer to Naomi's "field" or "parcel of land" (4:3, 5). The reader concludes that, despite the natural fertility of the land, Naomi encountered death and sterility in the *sadeh* of Moab. At the same time, Ruth, a native of "the country of Moab," helped her mother-in-law to find life in the *sadeh* of Judah!

The Risk

Elimelech's choice of Moab as the location of his sojourn presents problems to the reader of the book of Ruth, who is alert to the sharply differing attitudes toward Moab in other parts of the Old Testament.

A Negative View of Moab

In the days of the judges (Judg. 3:14), Saul (1 Sam. 14:47), David (2 Sam. 8:2), Jehoram of Israel (2 Kgs. 3:5), and Jehoiakim of Judah (2 Kgs. 24:2) Moab was an enemy of Israel. Only after the unsuccessful effort to prevent the migrating Israelites from crossing Moabite territory (Num. 22:4-6) did King Balak of Moab allow them passage (Deut. 2:29).

For this reason Moabites were excluded from the assembly of Israel forever (Deut. 23:4). An early ballad singer called them the "people of Chemosh" (Num. 21:29). The Moabite wives of Solomon brought the cult of Chemosh to Jerusalem (1 Kgs. 11:7, 33). According to George E. Mendenhall (*The Tenth Generation,* 111), the customs of human sacrifice and ritual sexual intercourse (cf. Jer. 3:1-2; 7:31) came into Israel from Moab at the time of Solomon's reign. Prophetic oracles spoke of Moab's pride and arrogance (Isa. 16:6; Jer. 48:29-30; cf. Amos 2:1; Zeph. 2:8). In the days of Ezra and Nehemiah, intermarriage with Moabite women was seen as the source of "abominations" in Israel (Ezra 9:1; Neh. 13:1).

The attitudes expressed in these passages suggest the great risk to Bethlehemites living, even temporarily, in the land of Moab.

A Positive View of the Moabites

According to one Deuteronomic tradition, God gave land to the Moabites because they were part of his plan for the region of Transjordan (Deut. 2:9). Moses was buried in Moab (Deut. 34:5-6). David put his mother and father under the protection of the king of Moab during his struggle with Saul (1 Sam. 22:3-4). Prophetic oracles that speak of the pride of Moab are at the same time laments over the devastation of Moab by Assyria or Babylon. The tears of the prophets echo God's grief that the "joy and gladness" of the harvest have been taken away from Moab. Their heart "throbs like a harp for Moab" (Isa. 16:9-11; cf. Jer. 48:31, 36). According to the oracle in Jer. 48, God's ultimate will, frustrated by the rebellious pride of Moab, was to "restore the fortunes of Moab in the latter days" (Jer. 48:47).

9

These texts give a different picture of Moab, which seems more compatible with the positive evaluation of Moab implied in the story of Ruth, who was herself a Moabite. This is one reason for locating the Narrator in the "golden age of Hebrew narrative" (see above, 2) before the disintegration of Solomon's later years that the historian blames on the corrupting influence of Moabite religion (1 Kgs. 11:1, 7). In fact, the book of Ruth is a bold challenge to readers in every age to open themselves to different evaluations of a foreign people usually considered as evil, even to the possibility that God could use a foreigner like Ruth in his plan for all nations! Readers will recall Jesus's high evaluation of Samaritans who were looked down on by Jews (Luke 10:33; 17:16-18; cf. John 4:5-9).

The Woman Alone

The brief opening paragraph of the story of Ruth presents Naomi as the survivor of a double disaster: a famine in Judah that made her family refugees among a people not their own, and the death in Moab of her husband and two sons. In patriarchal society, a widowed and childless woman was automatically marginalized by society. The story begins with a man (Heb. *ish*) and his wife (*ishto,* literally "his woman," 1:2). Ten years later the Narrator describes Naomi as neither wife (that is, "woman with a man") nor mother, but simply "the woman" (*ha-ishshah,* 1:5), alone and vulnerable in an alien world. Like Mother Zion in exile, Naomi "was bereaved and barren, exiled and put away . . . left all alone" (Isa. 49:21).

The phrase "was left" (Ruth 1:3, 5) presents Naomi as *the last remaining remnant* of Elimelech's family. The Hebrew verb translated "left" is the root of the noun translated "remnant." Naomi was like the widow who lamented that the death of her son would "quench my one *remaining* ember, and leave to my husband neither name nor *remnant* on the face of the earth" (2 Sam. 14:7).

In our time, when millions of refugees move across boundaries to escape hunger, war, and persecution, and when death destroys the hopes of many, Naomi the survivor is a very contemporary character. Of the twenty million refugees in today's world, 70 percent are women and children. Like Naomi, many are elderly. They are vulnerable to hunger, disease, or physical violence.

Naomi was, however, not only the sole *survivor* of her family; she was also a *sign of hope*. The bold affirmation of the book of Ruth is that Naomi "the woman" (Ruth 1:5), with neither husband nor sons, is in fact *the remnant who will return*. Her story is an illustration of the words of Isaiah, who named his son Shear-jashub, which means "a remnant shall return" (Isa. 7:3). Isaiah explained the meaning of this name when he told his people in the midst of a national crisis that "a remnant will return" (Isa. 10:21).

Readers of the book of Ruth in later years could see in Naomi a representative figure of "the *remnant* that is *left*" of God's people whom God will recover from many nations (Isa. 11:11; cf. Jer. 23:3). She was like "the surviving remnant of the house of Judah," which "shall again take root downward, and bear fruit upward" in the land (Isa. 37:31). Naomi was one of the "weak . . . low and despised in the world" (1 Cor. 1:27, 28) chosen by God "to be a part of the events and relationships which will shape history" (K. C. Abraham, "Eulogy and Mission").

THE RETURN OF THE REMNANT
Ruth 1:6-22

A DOUBLE MOVEMENT

After ten years in "the country of Moab," Naomi, the surviving remnant of her family, returned to Bethlehem, her hometown. The key word in Ruth 1:6-22 is Heb. *shub*, variously translated as "return" (1:6, 10, 15, 22), "turn back" (vv. 11, 12, 16), "go back" (vv. 7, 8, 15), "bring back" (v. 21), and "come back" (v. 22). The decisions of Naomi, Orpah, and Ruth are all about returning. In five instances this verb refers to a return to the Moabite hometowns of Orpah and Ruth. In six instances the verb describes Naomi's return to Bethlehem from Moab, in which Ruth joins her. The double movement of returning dominates this episode of the story: for Orpah it was back to Moab. Naomi, with Ruth at her side, went back to Bethlehem,

NAOMI'S CHOICE: EXODUS TO LIFE (1:6-7)

God's Time

It was the right time for Naomi's decision to return to her people. News had come that the LORD, who she believed had brought disaster (Ruth 1:13), "had visited his people and given them food" (v. 6 RSV). This was "good news from a far country" which came as "cold water to a thirsty soul" (Prov. 25:25). The "later rain" (Deut. 11:14) had fallen in November, and the barley and wheat crops had been planted. "The beginning of the barley harvest" (Ruth 1:22), which followed the Festival of Unleavened Bread in March or April, was at hand. It was time to gather

12

Yahweh's gift of "seed to the sower and bread to the eater" (Isa. 55:10).

The Hebrew word *paqad* (Ruth 1:6), translated "visit" in the RSV, refers to God's active intervention in human affairs, whether in judgment or in favor. So the psalmist asked "what are . . . mortals that you *care for* (KJV "visit") them?" (Ps. 8:4). Other translations of this word in Ruth 1:6 are "considered" (NRSV), "cared for" (NEB), "taken note of" (NJPS), or "blessed" (TEV).

The meaning of *paqad* in Ruth 1:6 is clarified in a beautiful psalm about God's care:

> You *visit* the earth and water it,
> you greatly enrich it;
> the river of God is full of water;
> you provide the people with grain,
> for so you have prepared it.
> You water its furrows abundantly,
> settling its ridges,
> softening it with showers,
> and blessing its growth.
>
> (Ps. 65:9-10)

The good news for Naomi was that Yahweh the LORD of the harvest had "visited" his people in Bethlehem once again. It was time to return.

An Initiative of Faith

With neither husband nor sons, Naomi decided on her own to return to Bethlehem. Two verbs, both used with the verb *shub*, emphasize Naomi's initiative. She "*started* to return" (Ruth 1:6) and "*set out* . . . to go back" (v. 7). The basic meaning of the Hebrew verb translated "started" *(qum)* is to rise up out of a condition of lethargy, sorrow, and discouragement. By this verb, the Narrator tells the reader that Naomi's response to the disasters was not passive acceptance, but a resolute initiative of faith. The words spoken by a prophet to the discouraged exiles in Babylon would fit Naomi's situation well:

13

Shake yourself from the dust, *rise up* . . .
    loose the bonds from your neck,
    O captive daughter of Zion!

(Isa. 52:2)

The second Hebrew verb *(yatsa')*, here translated "set out," means to go out or exit from one place in search of another. With various translations it describes the Exodus from Egypt to the Promised Land (Exod. 13:3-4; Deut. 4:45), as well as the "new Exodus" from Babylon to a new Jerusalem (Isa. 48:20; 52:11-12). The Narrator used this verb to suggest that Naomi was beginning her own "exodus" journey from death in Moab to life in Bethlehem.

Freedom of Choice

Naomi's freedom to decide on her own is not open to all. Sr. Mary Corona of India has written, "According to Sartre, freedom of choice is the essence of life. . . . If we go by this statement, very few women in India are alive. For the vast majority of women today, decisions great and small are made by others. . . . Except for a few, women even today are not aware of their dignity as persons and the possibility of a different way of being, a being of mutuality instead of subordinance" ("Worth," 62-64).

NAOMI'S ADVICE: "TURN BACK, MY DAUGHTERS"

Naomi was determined to return to Bethlehem by herself. She urged her daughters-in-law three times to "go back" (v. 8) or "turn back" (vv. 11, 12), and asked them, "Why will you go with me?" (v. 11). Perhaps she thought that her Moabite daughters-in-law would be a burden for a poor elderly widow to feed and house. To return to Bethlehem with her would mean, for them, hardship, poverty, and no chance of marrying younger brothers of their husbands according to the custom of levirate marriage (Deut. 25:5-6). Ruth was too old to have any more sons (Ruth 1:12-13). If, as she said, Yahweh's hand had turned against her (v. 13), it could turn against them too.

14

Security

When Naomi urged them to return each to her "mother's house" (v. 8), she probably meant that they could take a first step toward remarriage. Further, she expressed the faith that Yahweh would give them "security, each of you in the house of your husband" (v. 9). Readers may sense in Naomi's wish for her daughters-in-law more than the hope that they would get married. Implied by the word "security" is the wish that they should each find the answer to a universal human longing for a home where love, peace, and mutual respect for each other's dignity would nourish and uphold all family members. Significantly, Orpah chose the "security" of a home and family in Moab. Ruth gave up her own "security" in order to share Naomi's insecurity, but found "security" for them both.

The word translated "security" in Ruth 1:9 and 3:1 has several levels of meaning in the Bible. The verb form means to settle down after a period of wandering. The noun form means, literally, "rest" for the weary. During the wilderness period Yahweh would find a temporary "resting place" for his wandering people (Num. 10:33). Their permanent "rest" — that is, a place of peace and security from dangers round about — would be in the Promised Land (Josh. 1:13). Even in the land of Israel, however, Baruch complained that he was weary and could find no "rest" (Jer. 45:3).

As Naomi suggested, however, true "rest" is a gift of God. People of faith knew that God's presence is the source of this "rest" (Exod. 33:14). Whether in the wilderness on their way to the Promised Land (Deut. 12:9) or in exile from it (Lam. 1:3), the Israelites longed for this "rest." Prophetic words describe it beautifully:

> Then justice will dwell in the wilderness,
>   and righteousness abide in the fruitful field.
> The effect of righteousness will be peace,
>   and the result of righteousness, quietness and trust forever.
> My people will abide in a peaceful habitation,
>   in secure dwellings, and in quiet *resting* places.
>   (Isa. 32:16-18)

15

"Rest" as a gift of God is stressed in the New Testament. Jesus promised rest for those who "labor and are heavy laden" (Matt. 11:28 RSV). Rest is God's gift to those "who have believed" (Heb. 4:3). Yet it lies in the future, so that believers should "make every effort to enter that rest" (Heb. 4:11).

Covenant Love in Moab

Naomi's blessing on her two daughters-in-law reveals another important theological insight of the Narrator:

> May the LORD *deal kindly* with you, as you have dealt with the dead and with me. (Ruth 1:8)

The expression "deal kindly" literally means to "practice *hesed*."

Note on Hesed Hesed is a Hebrew word whose rich meaning makes it necessary to translate it in several different ways. In the OT it is most often associated with the covenant between Yahweh and his people. The term "steadfast love" is commonly used in the RSV and NRSV to refer to Yahweh's covenant love for his people, as in the statement that Yahweh is "abounding in steadfast love and faithfulness" (Exod. 34:6; cf. Ps. 136:1). When it describes the relationship between members of the covenant community, the terms "loyalty" (as in Prov. 3:3; Hos. 4:1) and "kindness" (as in 2 Sam. 9:1; Mic. 6:8) are often used. Yahweh expects his people to show "steadfast love" toward him, in response to his "steadfast love" for them, as in the words of Yahweh quoted by Hosea: "I desire steadfast love and not sacrifice" (Hos. 6:6).

In the book of Ruth the word *hesed* appears in the phrase "deal kindly" (Ruth 1:8), and the words "kindness" (2:20) and "loyalty" (3:10). In this commentary we will use the terms "covenant love," "loyalty," "covenant loyalty," and "kindness." (For a full discussion of this term, see Katharine Doob Sakenfeld, *Faithfulness in Action,* chs. 1–3.)

Naomi praised her two Moabite daughters-in-law for their kindness *(hesed),* toward her two sons and, after their deaths, toward her. Where had Ruth and Orpah learned to practice *hesed?*

The implication is that the two Moabite women had learned about Yahweh's steadfast love and the human response of covenant loyalty from their years as members of a family that knew of Yahweh's steadfast love and were kind (practiced *hesed*) to one another.

Naomi further expressed the hope that, even after they had returned to their people and their gods, Yahweh would show them steadfast love *(hesed)* and help them to find "security" in the house of their husbands! We may conclude from Naomi's blessing on her Moabite daughters-in-law that, in the Narrator's view, the circle of Yahweh's steadfast love is as wide as the earth and is present among all peoples. This view was expressed clearly by a psalmist: "The earth is full of the steadfast love of the LORD" (Ps. 33:5). A prophet expressed both the beauty and the transiency of this virtue: "Their constancy *(hesed)* is like the flower of the field . . . the flower fades" (Isa. 40:6-7).

The practice of *hesed* is part of the social contract that holds society together. When it is lacking everything falls apart, as Hosea observed:

> There is no faithfulness or *loyalty*,
>   and no knowledge of God in the land.
> Swearing, lying, and murder,
>   and stealing and adultery break out;
>   bloodshed follows bloodshed.
> Therefore the land mourns,
>   and all who live in it languish.
>
>   (Hos. 4:1-3)

The Gods of Moab

Naomi also reminded her daughters-in-law that in returning to Moab they would, besides rejoining their own *people,* also go back to their *gods* (Ruth 1:15). Although the Hebrew word *elohim* may be translated by the singular "god," or the plural "gods," Naomi was probably thinking of local village or neighborhood gods or spirits, like those worshipped in Asian and African communities today. We might call them the gods of folk religions.

In this remark, Naomi showed her practical realism, as well as her real concern for her daughters-in-law. Even though Yahweh would be with them and show them steadfast love in Moab, they would no longer have the support of a group of Yahweh worshippers. Marriage into Moabite families and residence among people who followed Moabite folk religions would make it difficult for them to remember the First Commandment, which they would have learned from Naomi.

By way of example, a university student in northern Thailand told her professor that she had once declared her faith in Jesus Christ and been baptized while in secondary school. However, when her father, a government official, was assigned to work in another community where there were no Christians, she lost contact with the Christian faith and ceased to believe in God.

ORPAH'S CHOICE: RETURN TO MOAB (1:14)

Orpah kissed Naomi and followed her advice to "turn back . . . go your way" (v. 12). Naomi urged Ruth to follow her (v. 15), leaving Naomi in her bitterness, free to return by herself.

The Narrator does not condemn Orpah for her decision. However, readers of the story of Ruth may well think of Orpah's decision in two ways: it might mean a going back to the old ways of Moab, to the traditional culture and religion of Moab, to the people of Chemosh (see "A Negative View of Moab," 9). On the other hand, readers might think of Orpah's return to Moab as an opportunity for her to bring to her people a new vision of Yahweh's steadfast love and of human relations which she had seen as a member of this family that worshipped Yahweh. She might play a role like that of the young Israelite girl who served Naaman's wife (2 Kgs. 5:1-5).

RUTH'S CHOICE: BACK TO BETHLEHEM WITH NAOMI (1:16-18)

Ruth's decision is the direct opposite of Orpah's. She loved her mother-in-law so much that she refused to do her bidding! Instead of kissing Naomi and returning to her Moabite home, Ruth "*clung* to her" (1:14). As we see from Gen. 2:24, the word "cling" signifies the formation of a new unity binding both sides together. When Ruth stepped forward to "cling" to Naomi, she bound the lives of these two vulnerable widows together in a new solidarity.

A Radical Decision, and a Beautiful Vow

Ruth's beautiful vow expressing her radical decision is remarkable not only in its contrast to Orpah's decision, but also in the implications it had for Ruth herself. It meant a complete break with her past. At the same time, the Narrator's brief comment that Naomi, seeing Ruth's determination, "said no more to her" (Ruth 1:18) suggests that Naomi did not understand why this young Moabite woman would want to give up hopes of a home to follow her. She was still asking the question in her heart, "Why will you go with me? " (v. 11).

Your walk, my walk. Whereas Orpah had followed Naomi's advice to "go your way" back to Moab (Ruth 1:12), Ruth signified her decision to "go," or "walk" (another translation of the same Hebrew word), with Naomi (v. 16). It was now no longer "the woman" alone (v. 5), but mother and daughter walking side by side, sharing life together.

Your lodging, my lodging. Whereas Orpah had sought "security" in the house of a husband (v. 9), Ruth was ready to give up the "security" of a husband and family, spend nights ("lodge") on the way, enjoy her friendship, and help Naomi in her search for a new "security."

Your people, my people. Ruth's decision not to "leave" Naomi (1:16) meant that she had to "leave" her own people and native land (2:11) and bind herself to Naomi's people. She was like the disciples of Jesus who "left house . . . brothers . . . sisters . . . mother . . . father . . . children . . . fields for [Jesus'] sake and for the sake of the good news" (Mark 10:29).

Your God, my God. In contrast to Orpah who went back to "her gods" (Ruth 1:15), Ruth was ready to make an absolute commitment to the God Naomi had taught her to love. So, in addition to clinging to Naomi, she was ready to "cling" to Yahweh

(Ps. 63:8), thereby binding herself to Yahweh's covenant with Abraham, which extended to David and across the generations to Jesus Christ. Ruth is one of numerous other people in the Bible who declared their loyalty to Yahweh across cultural and religious lines: Jethro the Midianite (Exod. 18:11), Rahab the Canaanite (Josh. 2:11), Naaman the Syrian (2 Kgs. 5:15), foreign merchants from Egypt, Ethiopia, and Seba (Isa. 45:14), and the Ethiopian official (Acts 8:36). Ruth is like countless others across the ages who have made the costly decision to follow the "God of gods and LORD of lords" (Deut. 10:17).

Your burial place, my burial place. Orpah went back to her own people and would be buried there with her ancestors, but Ruth's solidarity with Naomi extended even to death and burial by her side, as foremothers of the people of Israel.

Ruth and Abraham

Ruth's bold decision to make new ties of kinship, family, country, and faith invites comparison with Abraham, who left his own country, his family, and his father's house (Gen. 12:1) in response to God's call. As Abraham and Sarah were founding father and mother of a new people, so Ruth was the founding mother of a new dynasty, and hence a link in the family line of the coming Messiah. However, in Ruth's case we know of no divine command. Unlike Abraham, she had to make the decision by herself to follow Naomi. She had no husband or retinue of servants to go with her. She was ready to accept insecurity because of her faith in Naomi's God.

A MODEL FOR TODAY

Today Ruth may be compared with women and men who cross cultural, racial, and regional boundaries to bind themselves with one another in faith-based covenantal relationships that look to the future with faith and hope. From India comes the challenge to people of faith to seek solidarity over against "communal frenzy" that can tear a people apart (Report of the Seventh Biannual Conference of the SCM of India).

After attending an ecumenical gathering in Seoul, Korea, a Thai woman wrote that she "found out who Christ was through ethnically and culturally diverse individuals. . . . We came to know Christ as the Lord who came into the world to meet us attired in the rich dress of our varied cultures, liberating us from those powers which divided us, reconciling us to Himself and one another, and forming us into community committed to peace, justice and the care of creation. . . . As a woman, I felt Christ being closer to us — women of this entire world not just a particular place" (Woranut Pantupong, "Reflections on Seoul — a Year Later").

ARRIVAL IN BETHLEHEM (1:19-22)

The Narrator emphasizes the return of Naomi and Ruth by repeating three times "they came to Bethlehem" (Ruth 1:19, 22). Yet what should have been a joyful homecoming was, instead, full of bitterness. In her words to the women of Bethlehem, Naomi made three complaints (vv. 20-21).

Bitterness

First, she stressed her bitterness of soul by using the Hebrew word for "bitter" three times: "It has been far more bitter *(mar)* for me than for you" (v. 13). "Call me Mara (bitter), for the Almighty has dealt bitterly *(mar)* with me" (v. 20). Bitterness like Naomi's appears frequently in the Old Testament. It is a very human form of anger, a complaint that life is not fair, and is found often in the Old Testament. The lives of *the slaves in Egypt* were made "bitter with hard service" (Exod. 1:14). *The people in the wilderness* "could not drink the water of Marah because it was bitter" (Exod. 15:23), *Rachel,* in a voice of "lamentation and bitter weeping," was grieving for her children, refusing "to be comforted . . . because they are no more" (Jer. 31:15). *King Hezekiah* could not sleep because of "the bitterness of my soul" (Isa. 38:15). *Jeremiah* wept bitterly when the enemy took his people captive in 597 B.C. (Jer. 13:17). At the fall of Tyre, *the merchants of the Mediterranean world* wept "in bitterness of soul, with bitter mourning" (Ezek. 27:31). *The people of Israel,* per-sonified as Mother Zion, complained that God "has filled me with bitterness . . . sated me with wormwood" (Lam. 3:15); *Job* protested "in the bitterness of my soul" (Job 7:11), that "the Almighty . . . made my soul bitter" (27:2). Readers can under-stand Naomi's bitterness of soul.

Yet the story of Ruth reminds us that bitterness is not the last word. Naomi will later praise Yahweh "whose kindness has not forsaken the living or the dead" (Ruth 2:20). King Hezekiah realized that his suffering was for his own "welfare" (Isa. 38:17). Mother Zion in her bitterness still believed that

> . . . The LORD will not reject forever.
> Although he causes grief, he will have compassion
>   according to the abundance of his steadfast love;
> for he does not willingly afflict
>   or grieve anyone.
>
> (Lam. 3:31-32)

Affliction

Second, Naomi complained that Yahweh had "dealt harshly" with her. This expression is a translation of a Hebrew verb *'anah,* which means basically to "answer," as in the petition "answer me, for I am poor and needy" (Ps. 86:1). When the answer is harsh, the meaning may be "to afflict," as in the threat that "the LORD will afflict you with consumption, fever . . ." (Deut. 28:22; cf. NIV translation of Ruth 1:21, "afflicted me"). Naomi's complaint was that when she cried to the LORD for an answer at the time of the death of her husband, Yahweh answered her with the death of her two sons. She could have used words from the Psalms like "I am lonely and afflicted" (Ps. 25:16), or "O my God, I cry by day, but you do not answer; and by night, but find no rest" (Ps. 22:2). Behind her complaints, however, would be the faith that Yahweh does "not despise or abhor the affliction of the afflicted" (Ps. 22:24).

Calamity

Third, Naomi blamed God for bringing "calamity" on her. She was not alone in this. Another translation of the verb is found in Moses' complaint that Yahweh had "mistreated" his people (Exod. 5:22). Elijah said the same thing about Yahweh's treatment of the widow: "O LORD my God, have you brought calamity even upon the widow with whom I am staying, by killing her son?" (1 Kgs. 17:20). Jeremiah compared Yahweh to a "deceitful brook, like waters that fail" (Jer. 15:18). Job spoke in the same way: "Surely now God has worn me out . . . shriveled me up . . . torn me in his wrath, and hated me" (Job 16:7, 8, 9).

Unrecognized Hope

Ironically, Naomi, perhaps completely wrapped up in her own suffering, did not even mention her Moabite daughter-in-law. The Narrator makes sure that the reader will not overlook the importance of "Ruth the Moabite, her daughter-in-law, who came back with her from the country of Moab" (Ruth 1:22). Naomi did not yet know that God's answer to her cries was in the Moabite woman who had clung to her and sworn to walk by her side on her return to Bethlehem. Ruth would cause "Mara" ("the bitter one") to become "Naomi" (the "lovely one") again. She would fill the void of emptiness in Naomi's heart with fullness, embody God's grace instead of harshness, and bring blessing in place of calamity. She would bring "hope for your future" (Jer. 31:17), and change her "mourning into dancing" (Ps. 30:11).

HARVEST JOY
Ruth 2:1-23

Chapter 2 tells how, at harvesttime in the fields of Bethlehem of Judah, the two poor widows found joy to replace bitterness and bounty to fill their emptiness. The harvest joy in this episode is similar to the song of Mary, another woman in the family line of the Messiah, who praised God, for "he has filled the hungry with good things" (Luke 1:53).

BOAZ

The Narrator begins the story of harvest joy by introducing the other main character, along with three facts about him that give the reader clues for understanding the rest of the story. After these three clues, the reader learns his name: Boaz.

Kinsman

First, he was Naomi's "kinsman" (NIV, REB, TEV "relative") on her husband's side. The Hebrew word used here is similar to that found in Ruth 3:2, "our kinsman Boaz," but not the same as the word translated "next-of-kin" (3:13). It could mean simply a "friend" (as in Job 19:14), known to Naomi through her husband. Here, however, the term surely implies a blood relationship. Kinship ties with Naomi are of great importance in the later development of the story.

A Man of Worth

Second, he was "a prominent rich man," or "a man of substance" (NJPS), a landowner who employed a large group of laborers in the harvest, and who was well able to be of help to the two poor widows who had just arrived. The Hebrew word *hayil*, here translated "rich," anticipates Boaz's use of the same word to describe Ruth as "worthy" (3:11). Perhaps the Narrator wished to suggest that Boaz's "worth" had a double meaning: he was "rich" both materially and morally. At the end of the story, the same word will be used in a wish that these two "worthy" partners should "prosper" in Bethlehem (literally, 'produce *hayil*'; 4:11 RSV).

Although there is no explicit reference to his age, we learn later that Boaz was older than "the young men" in his employ (cf. 3:10). The Narrator gives no hint about whether he was a widower (probable) or had been single all his life (unlikely). Jewish legend speculated that the funeral of his late wife coincided with the arrival of Ruth and Naomi from Moab.

Family Member

Finally, besides being a "kinsman" (that is, of the same clan), Boaz was "of the family of Elimelech," Naomi's late husband. The Hebrew term translated "family" *(mishpahah)* designates a kinship group larger than the immediate family unit or "father's house" *(bet ab)* and smaller than the clan or tribe. We may use the phrase "extended family." Boaz was a member of Elimelech's extended family *(mishpahah)* but not of his immediate family *(bet ab)*, which was in danger of extinction due to the death of both sons.

Membership in the extended family made Boaz a possible "redeemer" who could come to the aid of Naomi and her daughter-in-law. Family solidarity, one of the key concerns in the story of Ruth, is expressed in a cluster of words related to the concept of "the next-of-kin" (Heb. *go'el*). This noun is a participle of the verb *ga'al*, which carries the meaning of rescuing or delivering. It may also be translated "redeem." Thus the "next-of-kin" or "redeemer" (*go'el*) is the one bearing the responsibility for rescuing or redeeming the relative who is in difficulty. Another noun derived from the verb *ga'al* is *ge'ullah*, which means "the right of redemption" (Lev. 25:29; Jer. 32:7) or the act of getting back what had been lost, thus "redeeming" (Ruth 4:7).

The custom of "redemption" by a "redeemer" or "next-of-kin" was part of ancient Israel's system of social security based on the extended family and the tribe. If a member of the extended family had to sell land, the next-of-kin would buy it back to restore the property to the family (Lev. 25:25). If one sold oneself to an alien, the next-of-kin had the right and duty to restore the damage done to the family or tribe by paying the purchase price and setting the slave free (Lev. 25:47-49). If a person who had been wronged died, the restitution for the crime committed should be paid to the next-of-kin who acts on behalf of the whole family (Num. 5:8).

This helps us to see the significance of several references to this important custom. The Narrator's remark that Boaz was "of the [extended] family of Elimelech" (Ruth 2:1) alerts the reader to the possibility that he might be next-of-kin. Naomi's remark that Boaz was "one of our nearest kin" (v. 20) meant that she was not sure whether he was indeed "next-of-kin" or not. Ruth's challenge to Boaz, "you are next-of-kin" (3:9), meant that she was hoping that he was in fact Naomi's closest relative. Boaz replied that he was indeed a "near kinsman" but that there was "another kinsman more closely related than I" (3:12).

Following Lev. 19:18, 34 Jesus expanded this principle of family solidarity beyond the limits of the traditional family when he said that all those who do the will of God were his "brother and sister and mother" (Matt. 12:50). In the parable of the Good Samaritan, he extended family solidarity to the neighbor in need (Luke 10:36-37). In his description of the great judgment (Matt. 25:31-46), he extended family solidarity as an obligation of "all the nations" (v. 32) to come to the aid of those who are thirsty, hungry, stranger, naked, and in prison.

RUTH

Ruth, now a stranger in a new land, showed her determination to deal with the problem of hunger by her bold decision to go alone to glean in the fields of Bethlehem. The story does not tell us why Naomi did not go with her. We must assume that she was too old and weak to do so. Ruth, the young Moabite widow, made her own risky decision to go by herself to glean behind the reapers.

A Gleaner

Where poverty exists in any society, compassion, expressed through social custom or binding law, is necessary "so that the LORD your God may bless you in all your undertakings" (Deut. 24:19). The word "glean" is a key to ch. 2 of Ruth, where it appears twelve times (vv. 2, 3, 7, 8, 15 [twice], 16, 17 [twice], 18, 19, 23). The right to glean was part of the social contract, or covenantal obligation of landowners, and the privilege of the poor and the alien (Lev. 19:9-10). Without this compassionate provision for the poor, no initiative by Ruth would have enabled the two poor widows to survive.

Present-day "gleaning" can take many forms. Some churches operate food pantries or serve hot meals to the poor. Members may bring canned goods to church for stocking food pantries. Concerned people may collect donated food from supermarkets and distribute it to the poor in their community. Governments may make surplus food stocks available for low income families or individuals.

A Resident Alien

As long as Ruth was among her own people, the Narrator referred to her simply as "Ruth" (Ruth 1:14, 16). Elimelech and his family, on the other hand, went to "live" (Heb. *gur*) as temporary residents or resident aliens in Moab. On arrival in Bethlehem of Judah, however, the roles were reversed. Ruth became "the Moabite" (1:22; 2:2, 21), "who came back with Naomi from the country of Moab" (2:6). Even at the end of the story, Boaz still referred to his intended bride as "Ruth the Moabite" (4:5, 10).

Although the Hebrew word *ger*, usually translated "resident alien" or "sojourner," does not appear in the book of Ruth, it is clear that, as a Moabite in Israel, she would be classified as a *ger* or resident alien. She would not be accepted immediately by Israelite society, and could easily have been "alienated" from the mainstream. Aliens were at such risk in ancient Israelite society that numerous laws were made to protect them from oppression by powerful people (see, e.g., Lev. 19:33). The very existence of these laws suggests the vulnerability of aliens to oppression by the native-born Israelites.

Naomi's instruction to her daughter-in-law to "go out with his young women" (Ruth 2:22) shows her sensitivity to Ruth's vulnerability as a single woman in the harvest field. The Hebrew word translated "bother" is stronger than Boaz's word also translated "bother" in v. 9. Naomi's word implies violence, as may be seen in other translations: "touch" (KJV, NIV), "molest" (REB, TEV, JB). Rape was a possibility, as we see from the Deuteronomic law prescribing death to any man who "seizes and lies with" an engaged woman "in the open country" (Heb. *sadeh*), where there was no one to rescue her when she cried for help. That man would be like someone who "attacks and murders a neighbor" (Deut. 22:25-27). The reader is relieved to learn that Ruth kept herself from danger by staying close to Boaz's female laborers (Ruth 2:22).

Ruth is easily recognizable today as a vulnerable woman in a world dominated by men. In all parts of our world women are the poorest of the poor, the most economically marginalized, and unfairly burdened by global economic crises. Moreover, women are often victims of physical assault and degradation by rape, a problem that has become more acute in wars and conflict situations (Aruna Gnanadason, *No Longer a Secret*, 5).

Ruth is also a very contemporary figure as an alien in a foreign land. Today refugees from war and disaster cross boundaries into countries and cultures not their own. People of different cultures who used to live peacefully as neighbors suddenly find themselves enemies. Muslims may find themselves living among Buddhists as in Myanmar; Roman Catholics among Protestants as in Northern Ireland; Orthodox among Muslims as in Bosnia; Hindus among Muslims as in Pakistan. Members of one tribe may find themselves in hostile territory if they have to migrate because of famine. "Each verse of this story," says Lynne Bundesen, "should be examined by women who feel alienated, adrift, hungry, unloved" (*The Woman's Guide to the Bible*, 97).

OPPORTUNITY FOR COVENANT LOYALTY (2:3-13)

The beautiful harvest scene depicted in these verses focuses on Ruth and Boaz, but behind the scene is the hidden hand of Yahweh, creating an opportunity for human freedom to express covenant loyalty in action. Ruth's covenant loyalty to Naomi meant going to the fields (Ruth 2:3), asking permission of the foreman to glean behind the harvesters, and working hard from early morning to glean behind the reapers (v. 7).

Providence or Blind Chance?

The phrase "as it happened" (v. 3) is the Narrator's way of suggesting that what could not have been planned or foreseen by humans, and seems therefore to be simply good or bad "luck" or "fate," came about by divine providence. The word translated "happened" carries an ambiguity, since it can also be translated "chance" (1 Sam. 6:9) or "fate" (Eccl. 3:19). The Narrator does not say that God actually directed Ruth's steps to Boaz's field, but the implication is there because this encounter is essential to the eventual outcome of the story. God's part was to provide an *opportunity* for Ruth and Boaz to interact, without controlling their actions.

The Narrator's statement that Ruth "happened" to arrive at Boaz's field opens our understanding to the possibility that the hand of a loving God may be present in the events of our lives, providing opportunities to act according to God's will, even though we may feel, like Naomi, that God has turned against us.

Greetings and Their Meaning

With this in mind we can look again at Boaz's greeting to the reapers and their reply. On the surface, "The LORD be with you" (Ruth 2:4), is simply a routine greeting, like "good morning" or "hello." If we look below the surface, however, the wish that Yahweh will be "with" them means that they must be open to God's hidden hand to correct, support, and direct their steps at all times. "When you turn to the right or when you turn to the left, your ears will hear a word behind you, saying, 'This is the way; walk in it' " (Isa. 30:21). They would gladly follow Yahweh's leading along "right paths" and say with the psalmist, "I fear no evil; for *you are with me*" (Ps. 23:4). They would rejoice in the words of the prophet to the exiles:

When you pass through the waters, *I will be with you;*
    and through the rivers, they shall not overwhelm you;
when you walk through fire, you shall not be burned,
    and the flame shall not consume you.

                                                             (Isa. 43:2)

The apparently simple greeting "the LORD be with you" is in fact a profound statement of faith that God who dwells "in the high and holy place" is also "*with* those who are contrite and humble in spirit, to revive the spirit of the humble, and to revive the heart of the contrite" (Isa. 57:15). This is the meaning of the name Immanuel, "God with us" (Isa. 7:14). It is the substance of Jesus' promise to be with his followers (Matt. 28:20).

"The LORD bless you." By this greeting (Ruth 2:4), the reapers asked Yahweh to bless Boaz as he had blessed Noah and his sons (Gen. 9:1) and, through them, all humankind (v. 19). They were saying that the blessing promised to Abraham and through him to "all the families of the earth" (12:3) would be effective in the life of Boaz. The effect of the blessing on Boaz would be to "make you abound in prosperity, in the fruit of your womb, in the fruit of your livestock, and in the fruit of your ground. . . ." Accordingly, the LORD would "open for you his rich storehouse, the heavens, to give the rain of your land in its season and to bless you in all your undertakings" (Deut. 28:11-12). It would include the wish that Boaz would conduct his life with covenant loyalty in order that God's blessing would continue (cf. Deut. 28:13-14). Of particular interest to the development of the story is the implied wish that God would bless Boaz with offspring.

DIALOGUE IN THE FIELDS OF BOAZ

As in ch. 1, where the speeches of Naomi and Ruth are of major importance to the development of the story, so now in ch. 2 the dialogue between Boaz and Ruth carries the plot further and helps define the character of each of them.

Boaz: "Listen, My Daughter" (2:8-9)

Boaz first asked his harvesters about the strange "young woman" in his fields (Ruth 2:5). On learning that she had come from Moab with Naomi the widow of Elimelech, he welcomed her warmly as "my daughter" (v. 8), and urged her to stay with other "young women" in his field and gather behind his reapers. Sensing her vulnerability as an alien and a widow, he offered her protection from indecent advances of the male harvesters, and responded to her physical needs by inviting her to quench her thirst from the jars of water filled by his "young men" (v. 9). Later he gave her extra grain and told her to eat her fill at mealtime (v. 14). Further, he instructed the reapers to "pull out some handfuls for her from the bundles" for her to glean (v. 16).

Ruth: "I Am a Foreigner" (2:10)

Ruth responded to Boaz's kindness with joyful surprise that he had shown her such favor in fulfillment of her wish to Naomi (2:2). She explained this "favor" by saying that he had taken notice of her "when I am a foreigner." The Hebrew words translated "take notice" and "foreigner" come from the same root *nakar*, which means to "recognize" or "pay attention to." The same word appears in 3:14, where it means that one person could not "recognize" the other before the light of dawn.

The word *nokriya*, here translated "foreigner," is the feminine form of the noun *nokri* and means a woman who cannot be recognized as belonging to one's own group, and is therefore a stranger. A "foreign woman" was not subject to the protection of laws regarding "aliens" (*ger*). More than that, the word *nokriya* was ambiguous. From popular proverbs we learn that it could

31

carry connotations of immorality. The same word may be translated "loose woman" (Prov. 2:16) or "adulteress." Young men
were taught that wisdom would "preserve [one] from the wife
of another, from the smooth tongue of the *adulteress (nokriya),*"
who "stalks a man's very life" (Prov. 6:24, 26; cf. 5:20; 7:5). It
is even possible, as some modern commentators suggest, that
Ruth as a "foreign woman" might be associated with "an ag-
gressive form of seduction and with the taint of idolatry" (Amy-Jill
Levine, "Ruth," 79).

The verb "take notice" expresses the joyful surprise of Ruth
(Ruth 2:10) and later of Naomi (2:19) that Boaz had not simply
labelled her as a "foreign woman" *(nokriya)* to be rejected or
exploited, but had "recognized" *(nakar)* her as a person of worth
in her own right (see Robert L. Hubbard, Jr., *The Book of Ruth,*
184). The reader will be reminded of Jesus' way of taking notice
of people. He said to Nathanael, "I saw you under the fig tree
before Philip called you" (John 1:48).

Boaz: "May the LORD Reward You"

In his second speech (Ruth 2:11-12), Boaz told Ruth why he
had taken notice of the "foreign woman" whose steps God had
directed to glean in his field. He saw in her a person with covenant
loyalty toward Naomi in words that recall Abraham: "how you
left your father and mother and your native land and came to a
people that you did not know before" (2:11; cf. Gen. 12:1). Ruth
the Moabite, who had said to Naomi "your people shall be my
people" (Ruth 1:16), had done this not for herself but for her
mother-in-law, even though, after the death of her husband, she
could have gone back to her people.

Boaz welcomed her with the wish that her acts of love would
bring a "full reward" (Ruth 2:12) from Yahweh, whom she had
accepted as her own God (1:16). The reader is left to wonder
what this reward might be — food for the hungry, or something
more?

The expression used by Boaz to describe Ruth as one who had
"come for refuge" under the "wings of the LORD, the God of
Israel" occurs frequently in the Psalms to describe Yahweh's

protection from surrounding dangers ("the destroying storms," Ps. 57:1) or from terror and disease (Ps. 91:4-6). Because of this kind of help, a psalmist will "sing for joy" in the shadow of Yahweh's wings (Ps. 63:7). Ruth the foreigner need not fear, because "all people may take refuge in the shadow of your [Yahweh's] wings" (Ps. 36:7). Jesus used a similar figure of speech to describe his loving concern for the people of Jerusalem, even though they rejected it (Matt. 23:37; Luke 13:34).

Ruth: "You Have Comforted Me" (2:13)

In her reply Ruth voiced the wish to continue to "find favor" in Boaz's sight, but went on to suggest a change of status for herself. In her words "you have comforted me," she used the simple first person pronoun "me." She could have used the same grammatical form in the second expression by saying "spoken kindly to *me.*" Instead, she used an ordinary polite expression for a subordinate woman in addressing her superior, "your [female] servant" (Heb. *shiphhah*). By using this word again in the last part of the sentence, "even though I am not one of your [female] servants," Ruth made the subtle suggestion that she would like to become one of Boaz's female servants or slaves, instead of a poor gleaner in his fields. One translation makes this suggestion explicit: "Would indeed that I were one of your [female] servants" (NAB). Ruth had accepted his words as making possible a change of status, from "foreign woman" *(nokriya)* to "[female] servant" *(shiphhah),* or "maid," like the "female slaves" of Abraham's household (Gen. 12:16) or Laban's "maid" Zilpah (Gen. 29:24).

The attentive reader, anticipating the further development of the story, is entitled to ask whether Ruth had a further change of status in mind. This leads to a consideration of the two words used by Ruth to describe the effect of Boaz's second speech (Ruth 2:13).

The word "comfort" (Heb. *naham*) in this case does not have its usual meaning of consolation, which might have been given to Ruth for the loss of her husband (cf. Gen. 37:35). Mahlon's death had occurred some time previously. It meant, rather, encouragement given to a "foreign woman" who was in great difficulty (note "you have given me courage," Ruth 2:13 JB). It meant an assurance of help to an alien widow that would change despair to confidence. Joseph "reassured" *(naham)* his brothers with the promise to "provide for you and your little ones" (Gen. 50:21). The promise that Yahweh would "comfort" the "waste places" of Zion meant that Yahweh would help the people make their war-ravaged countryside into a garden land again, and that "joy and gladness" would "be found in her, thanksgiving and the voice of song" (Isa. 51:3). "Comfort" means practical assistance, as in the prayer of the psalmist:

> Show me a sign of your favor,
>> so that those who hate me may see it and be put to shame,
> because you, LORD, have helped me and comforted me.
>> (Ps. 86:17)

Ruth's statement that Boaz had "comforted" her, meant that he had given her hope of a real change in her life situation.

The Hebrew expression translated "speak kindly" or "gently" (NIV, TEV) means literally to "speak to the heart," and carries a delightful ambiguity. On the one hand, it may suggest that Boaz spoke encouraging words like those of Joseph to his brothers (Gen. 50:21), David to his troops (2 Sam. 19:7), and Hezekiah to the temple workers (2 Chr. 30:22). On the other hand, it may imply the language of love, like the words of Shechem to Dinah (Gen. 34:3), a husband to his estranged wife (Judg. 19:3), or, by analogy, of Yahweh to his people (Isa. 40:2; Hos. 2:14, in each case translated "speak tenderly"). When Ruth said that Boaz had spoken directly to her heart, did she mean that she had heard in his remarks words of tenderness and affection, no matter how disguised? Did the Narrator intend to suggest further developments to his readers?

Boaz acknowledged this word of Ruth by inviting her to "come here," that is, near to him at the meal (Ruth 2:14). God created the opportunity for Ruth to meet Boaz, but Boaz's generous openness and Ruth's bold initiative showed their readiness to grasp the God-given opportunity.

A MODEL OF COVENANT LOYALTY

Boaz's covenant loyalty makes him a model Israelite. He was acting according to covenant commands to let "the resident aliens, the orphans, and the widows in your towns . . . come and eat their fill so that the LORD your God may bless you in all that you undertake" (Deut. 14:29), and to "open your hand to the poor and needy neighbor in your land" (Deut. 15:11). He would not "let loyalty *(hesed)* and faithfulness forsake" him (Prov. 3:3). He loved "kindness" *(hesed)* and did "justice" (Mic. 6:8).

Boaz's open-hearted generosity stands in sharp contrast to the description by the prophets of the greediness of those who "trample on the needy, and bring to ruin the poor of the land" (Amos 8:4), drive out "the women of my people . . . from their pleasant houses . . ." (Mic. 2:9), yet "lean upon the LORD and say, 'Surely the LORD is with us! No harm shall come upon us'" (Mic. 3:11). Boaz was not like the "perverse" evildoers who "eat up my [God's] people as they eat bread, and do not call upon God" (Ps. 53:3, 4). He was not "insolent" or "ruthless" (Ps. 54:3), nor did he "greedily devour human prey" (57:4). He did not "enter the path of the wicked" (Prov. 4:14), nor was his speech "crooked" or "devious" (v. 24).

HARVEST JOY (2:17-23)

Ruth's "reward" in fulfillment of Boaz's wish (Ruth 2:12) was a generous portion of barley to sustain Naomi and herself. An "ephah" was a dry measure weighing between 10 to 14 kg. (20-30 lbs.). This would have been enough food for ten to fourteen days for one person, or five to seven days for two. A day's wage for the reapers, according to documents from the time, would have been about 1 kg. of grain.

The Hard Work of Gleaning (2:17-18)

The "reward" was for hard work. Ruth had to bend down for long hours to *pick up* the ears of barley left by the reapers. Then she *beat them out* to separate the husks from the kernels. Next she *collected* the precious grain in her shawl, slung it over her shoulders, and *carried* it into Bethlehem. Finally she fulfilled her purpose of going to the fields by *giving* it to Naomi, along with "what was left over" of the parched grain from her noon meal. She held nothing back for herself.

We can imagine Ruth at work each day during the seven-week period from the Festival of Unleavened Bread marking the beginning of the barley harvest in April to the Festival of Weeks marking the end of the wheat harvest in June. We can see her bending down, picking up, beating out, gathering, and carrying the daily gleaning back to Naomi. Perhaps we might also think of her joining in a harvest song:

> The earth has yielded its increase;
>> God, our God, has blessed us.
> May God continue to bless us;
>> let all the ends of the earth revere him.

> (Ps. 67:6-7)

Naomi: "Blessed Be He by the LORD"

Upon Naomi's arrival in Bethlehem she had complained bitterly against the Almighty (Ruth 1:20-21). When Ruth reported the name of the kind landowner, however, Naomi's complaint turned to praise for Yahweh "whose kindness *(hesed)* has not forsaken the living or the dead" (2:20). Her joy was increased when she learned that Boaz had included "Ruth the Moabite" in his circle of care by urging her to "stay close" to his workers (v. 21; cf. v. 8). By the Narrator's careful design, this reported word of Boaz translates the same Hebrew word as that used in the statement that Ruth "clung" to Naomi (1:14). Boaz, the relative of Naomi, was inviting "Ruth the Moabite," the poor foreigner, to join his harvesting group and to share the benefits of "all my harvest" (2:21). When Naomi saw the pile of barley that Ruth laid at her feet, her first reaction was to thank Yahweh that the owner of the field where Ruth had gleaned had taken "notice" of her (2:19). Boaz's taking "notice" of her daughter-in-law meant to Naomi that Ruth was no longer a stranger or an alien. Words of a psalmist reflect Naomi's feelings:

> Hungry and thirsty,
>> their soul fainted within them.
> Then they cried to the LORD in their trouble,
>> and he delivered them from their distress; . . .
> Let them thank the LORD for his steadfast love,
>> for his wonderful works to humankind.
> For he satisfies the thirsty,
>> and the hungry he fills with good things.
>>> (Ps. 107:5-6, 8-9)

Ruth was like the "Gentiles by birth," who through Christ were "no longer strangers and aliens, but . . . citizens with the saints and also members of the household of God" (Eph. 2:11, 19).

The Living and the Dead

Naomi's words had further significance. When she praised her daughters-in-law for the "kindness" (hesed) they had shown to their father-in-law and their husbands and to Naomi herself, she was referring to their covenant love while those now dead were still alive (Ruth 1:8). Here, when Naomi referred to Yahweh's kindness to "the living and the dead" (2:20), she could not have meant simply the pile of barley that Ruth had brought to her. That would be of no use to "the dead."

The phrase meant that somehow the interests of the dead continue with the living, and that the unresolved problem following the deaths of her husband and her two sons would find its resolution in the living matrix of succeeding generations of children's children. This continuity is part of God's plan in choosing and calling a people whose vitality must be preserved from generation to generation. Naomi's remark that Boaz, introduced by the Narrator as "a relative" (2:1), was "one of our nearest kin" (2:20) implies that Boaz himself was part of God's "kindness" toward "the dead" as well as the living (Naomi and Ruth).

37

. . . WHERE YOU LODGE

The Narrator closes this episode with the comment that Ruth "lived with her mother-in-law," thus fulfilling her vow to lodge with Naomi instead of seeking the company of others of her own age. During the seven weeks of the harvest when the two women lived together, they must have recalled Boaz's blessing, "May you have a full reward from the LORD, the God of Israel, under whose wings you have come for refuge!" (2:12). Naomi was already making plans to make the blessing-wish come true.

A DARING ENCOUNTER
Ruth 3:1-18

In ch. 2 the generous portion of grain from Ruth's gleaning meant food for the hungry. In this chapter the heap of grain on Boaz's threshing floor is the setting for a secret encounter between Ruth and Boaz, arranged by Naomi. This encounter would set events in motion that would open the future for Ruth and Naomi, the family of Elimelech, and indeed the whole nation of Israel.

NAOMI'S PLAN (3:1-5)

A New Initiative

Ruth showed bold initiative in going to glean in the field of Boaz to enable the two impoverished women to survive (2:2). Now Naomi takes the initiative in order to bring about the fulfillment of her petition that Yahweh would show his "kindness" (*hesed*) by granting each of her daughters-in-law "security . . . in the house of your husband" (1:9; see 15). Here, her words "I need to seek some security for you" (3:1), parallel that prayer. Naomi did not wait passively for Yahweh to "grant security," but she herself became the means of seeking the security that was Yahweh's will.

The Right Time: Now!

With the word "now" (3:2), Naomi seized the opportunity provided by the harvest — Boaz would be "winnowing barley *tonight* at the threshing floor" (3:2). Her daring plan calling for immediate action reminds us of Paul's words to the Corinthians: "See, *now* is the acceptable time; see, *now* is the day of salvation!" (2 Cor. 6:2).

The Goal

Naomi's wish for her daughter was not only that she find "security," but that "it may be well (Heb. *tob*) with you." We learn from Deuteronomy, where this phrase occurs frequently, that "well-being" *(tob)* depends on all members of a family living according to God's commandments (Deut. 4:40; 5:29; 6:3). They must do "what is right and good in the sight of the LORD," (6:18), honor parents (5:16), and show kindness to other living creatures (22:7). Naomi was not merely seeking a husband for Ruth. She was hoping to help her establish a family where things would "go well." This meant finding a partner who would care for, be kind to, and respect the dignity of his foreign, vulnerable wife and their children, and be concerned with the welfare of the entire community.

The Plan

Naomi's instructions to Ruth are full of ambiguous, even provocative words that emphasize the daring nature of her plan. For readers familiar with other parts of the OT, the advice to "anoint yourself" (Ruth 3:3) evokes thoughts of Esther's treatment with "oil of myrrh . . . perfumes and cosmetics" to make her attractive to the king (Esth. 2:12). Readers may recall the account of the unfaithful wife who, while her husband was away on a journey, had "perfumed my bed with myrrh, aloes, and cinnamon" to attract her lover to her home to "take our fill of love until morning" (Prov. 7:17-18). These associations lead the reader to wonder whether Naomi was suggesting that Ruth prepare herself by perfume and attractive clothing for an actual sexual encounter! The place of the encounter also carried risk. In Israelite tradition, the threshing floor was not only the place of harvest, but also of immoral practices of the fertility cult (Hos. 9:1). At harvest-time men and women would come together on the threshing floor as a way of stimulating powers of fertility (the foreign deities Baal and Asherah) to ensure good crops and increase of flocks and herds. This helps us understand Naomi's instructions to Ruth not to make herself known to Boaz until he had finished eating and drinking (Ruth 3:3), and Boaz's remark that "it must not be known that the woman came to the threshing floor" (3:14). She might be suspected of immorality

More specifically, the encounter took place beside the "heap of grain." A sensitive reader will detect a hidden erotic allusion to the phrase "heap of wheat" as a description of a lover's body (Cant. 7:2). Furthermore, in the context of the threshing floor, Naomi's expression "lie" or "lie down" (Heb. *shakab*) describing the prone position of both Boaz and Ruth by the heap of grain (Ruth 3:4) would also stir the imagination of the reader. To "lie *with*" meant sexual embrace, whether the partners were married (Gen. 30:16) or not (Exod. 22:15). When reading Naomi's instructions that Ruth "lie down" at Boaz's feet, one might think of the example of the sons of Eli who "lay with the women who served at the entrance to the tent of meeting" (1 Sam 2:22). The reader senses the bold risk in Naomi's plans.

Finally, the phrase "uncover his feet" (Ruth 3:4) directs the reader to the expression "uncover the nakedness" that refers to incestuous sexual relations (Lev. 18:6-18). The Hebrew term translated "feet" (Ruth 3:4, 7) or "(the place of) his feet" (3:14) is derived from the ordinary word for "foot" *(regel)*, which, in the plural, sometimes means "legs" (1 Sam. 17:6). It is also a euphemism for sexual organs, referring to a man's private parts (Exod. 4:25; Isa. 7:20) or the "body" of the seraphim (Isa. 6:2 REB, TEV). The related Hebrew expression translated "offering yourself" (Ezek. 16:25) seems to be a literal reference to a woman opening her legs for sexual embrace. Readers of Ruth would wonder just how much of Boaz's lower body was to be uncovered!

Yet despite the risk, Naomi's plan was designed to bring about positive results. It depended on the character of both Ruth and Boaz. Ruth's full acceptance of the plan shows her willingness to take risks and her confidence in the covenant loyalty of Boaz.

The Encounter (3:6-13)

Ruth's Daring Action (3:6-7)

This part of the story is told with a minimum of comment, which heightens the dramatic excitement of the scene. Nothing is said about the probable festival background of the words "when Boaz had eaten and drunk" (Ruth 3:7). Had Boaz participated in the communal meal marking the end of the fifty-day period between the beginning of the barley harvest and the end of the wheat harvest that was celebrated at the Festival of Weeks (Exod. 34:22; Deut. 16:10)? There is no mention of the festive crowd at the threshing floor celebrating the "joy at the harvest" (Isa. 9:3) and raising "the shout over . . . your grain harvest" (Isa. 16:9). There is only the briefest hint (Ruth 3:14) that women other than Ruth might have been waiting for partners at the threshing floor (cf. Hos. 9:1). We do not know whether the custom was then in practice that, at the Festival of Weeks, all males would dance around the altar singing Pss. 113–118 (see J. Coert Rylaarsdam, "Weeks, Feast of"). However, those who read or heard the book of Ruth at festival time would think of verses from those songs that were related to the drama of that night:

> He raises the poor from the dust,
>   and lifts the needy from the ash heap,
> to make them sit with princes,
>   with the princes of his people.
> He gives the barren woman a home,
>   making her the joyous mother of children!
>
> (Ps. 113:7-9)

> May the Lord give you increase,
>   both you and your children.
> May you be blessed by the Lord,
>   who made heaven and earth.
>
> (Ps. 115:14-15)

The LORD protects the simple;
　when I was brought low, he saved me.
Return, O my soul, to your rest,
　for the LORD has dealt bountifully with you.

(Ps. 116:6-7)

The Narrator shows us a woman wrapped in a shawl, watching closely from the shadows to identify a particular man among the others. There he was! She watched him as he moved away from the crowd and went to lie down at the end of a large heap of winnowed grain. This was a great stroke of luck! The heap of grain would allow maximum privacy for Ruth to carry out Naomi's plan.

Naomi had instructed Ruth to wait until Boaz had "finished eating and drinking" (Ruth 3:3). The Narrator adds that he was "in a contented mood" before lying down (v. 7). The phrase "contented mood" means literally that he had "a sense of well-being," using the Hebrew word *tob*. By looking at the Hebrew root of the expression and relating it to similar expressions in Deuteronomy, we may conclude that, in a wider covenantal context, Boaz's sense of well-being *(tob)* was not only the result of a full stomach, but also the fruit of covenant obedience, and that he would make things go "well" *(tob)* with Ruth (see above, 37).

As soon as the man was asleep, the waiting woman moved "stealthily" to his side. The use of this rare Hebrew verb would associate her boldness with the cool courage of Jael, who moved "softly" to the sleeping Sisera (Judg. 4:21, using the same Hebrew word)! There, at the end of the heap of grain, she uncovered the "feet" or "legs" *(margelot)* of the sleeping man and lay down there, under his cloak, just as Naomi had instructed her. The Narrator emphasizes the sexual nature of the midnight encounter by speaking only of "the man" and "a woman" without use of names (Ruth 3:8), evoking thoughts of the first pair in the Garden of Eden (Gen. 2:23). Readers remember thankfully that Boaz was "a worthy man" (Ruth 2:1), who would not take advantage of Ruth.

Boaz: "Who Are You?" (3:8)

Suddenly "the man" woke up and was "startled," aware of the implicit danger in the presence of "a woman" at his feet. Could she be a prostitute looking for a partner? How would he protect his reputation? Never suspecting that Ruth would be there, his question, "Who are you?" is full of alarm and suspicion.

Ruth: "Marry Me!" (3:9)

In her reply "the woman" used her own name for the first time in the narrative: "I am Ruth!" She did not identify herself as "the young woman" who worked among the harvesters (2:5), "the Moabite who came back with Naomi" (2:6)," or the "foreigner" in Israelite society (2:10). She was the very person Boaz had "comforted" and to whose heart he had spoken kind words when they had first met in the fields of Bethlehem.

By giving her personal name first, she emphasized her dignity as a woman. By adding the expression "your servant" she showed a proper deference to Boaz as her benefactor. We should note that the word translated "servant" *(amah)* is different from the one Ruth used in her reply to Boaz in 2:13 (*shiphhah,* also translated "servant"). These terms are generally used as synonyms to refer to female slaves belonging to a wealthy person. The same terms are used in deferential speech by a woman to her social superior (see, e.g., 2 Sam. 14:4-17, where the wise woman of Tekoa speaks of herself as David's "servant" [*shiphhah*] six times in vv. 6, 7, 12, 15, 17, 19, and his "servant" [*amah*] twice in vv. 15, 16). Readers will nevertheless wonder about the Narrator's intention when he had Ruth use the word *amah* in this case. Two texts will be of help.

Abigail at first called herself David's "servant" (*amah,* 1 Sam. 25:24). However, when he sent to take her as his wife (*ishshah,* 1 Sam. 25:40), she said "your (female) servant" (*amah*) is a "(female) slave" (*shiphhah*) to wash the feet of "your (male) servants" (v. 41). In calling herself first of all David's *amah* who would be willing to do the work of a *shiphhah,* Abigail may have been accepting his invitation to become his wife (*ishshah*). This

44

suggests that the *amah*, as household servant, might be elevated to the position of wife. It is noteworthy that Hagar continued to be Sarah's "slave-girl" *(shiphhah)* even after she gave her temporarily to Abraham "as a wife" *(ishshah*, Gen. 16:3, 6). Although Rachel and Leah gave their "maids" *(shiphhah)* to Jacob "as a wife" *(ishshah*, Gen. 30:4, 9) only to beget children, it is clear that the two maids still belonged to their mistresses (cf. Ps. 123:2).

Queen Bathsheba, perhaps to distinguish herself from the "maids" *(shiphhah)* of the Genesis texts, referred to herself deferentially as David's "servant" *(amah*, 1 Kgs. 1:13, 17). By contrast, the medium of Endor showed her inferior status by calling herself Saul's "servant" *(shiphhah*, 1 Sam. 28:21, 22).

In the Ruth story, there may well be a distinction between the two Hebrew terms, which we may distinguish as "female slave" and "household servant." Thus, Ruth hoped at first to be accepted as Boaz's female slave *(shiphhah*, Ruth 2:13). When, on the threshing floor, she called herself his household servant *(amah)*, she was by implication suggesting her eligibility to become his wife (see Edward F. Campbell, Jr., *Ruth*, 101).

This implication is borne out by Ruth's request that Boaz "spread your cloak over your servant" (Ruth 3:9). Ruth's act of lifting the cover over Boaz's feet (probably his cloak) and covering herself with it was probably a dramatic request that she be taken under his protection as his wife *(ishshah)*. The dynamic equivalent of the phrase "spread your cloak" is, according to one translation, "marry me" (TEV). The phrase recalls Ezekiel's imaginative description of Yahweh's action when he found Israel as a young woman in the wilderness: "I spread the edge of my cloak over you . . . and entered into a covenant with you" (Ezek. 16:8).

In Boaz's blessing-wish (Ruth 2:12), the Hebrew word *kanaph* meant the "wings" of Yahweh that symbolize protection and care. By having Ruth use the same Hebrew word, here translated as "cloak," the Narrator implies that Ruth was asking Boaz to fulfill his own expressed wish for her. Boaz's "cloak" *(kanaph)* would be a symbol and sign of Yahweh's protecting "wings" *(kanaph)*. Ruth was suggesting that Boaz, by covering her with his "cloak" in marriage, would be giving her the protection of Yahweh's "wings"!

Finally, Ruth appealed to Boaz's sense of family solidarity: "for you are next-of-kin" *(go'el)*. By using this term, Ruth expanded the encounter beyond the realm of man-woman relationships into the wider field of family solidarity (see above, 24-26). By calling Boaz "next-of-kin," Ruth showed that her primary motivation was not self-gratification, but rather the desire to help rescue Naomi and the family of Elimelech from extinction. Ruth's words contrast sharply with the lustful words of Potiphar's wife to Joseph: "Lie with me!" (Gen. 39:12).

Ruth showed herself to be a model "Israelite woman," according to Athalya Brenner. She was "motivated neither by pleasure-seeking nor by financial or social ambitions." She was willing to "risk whatever little social status" she might have "in order to perpetuate the continuity of Judahite leader stock" (Althalya Brenner, *The Israelite Woman*, 108).

Boaz: "I Will Do All You Ask" (3:10-13)

Boaz's reply to Ruth is the longest speech in the entire story, and is worth study for its portrayal of right human relations in the family system of ancient Israel.

Blessed by the LORD (3:10). First, by asking for Yahweh's blessing on Ruth, Boaz said in effect that her actions and her request were approved by Yahweh. Her "loyalty" *(hesed)* was her response to Yahweh's "kindness" *(hesed)* that "has not forsaken the living or the dead" (2:20; cf. 1:8). In fact, "this last instance" of Ruth's "loyalty" (3:10) was a continuation of her earlier loyalty, when she left her own people, land, and gods, to go with Naomi (1:16-17; 2:11). The Narrator implies that Yahweh's "blessing" would be the "full reward from the LORD, the God of Israel, under whose wings you have come for refuge" (2:12).

Ruth showed her covenant loyalty in her choice of a member of Naomi's extended family *(mishpahah),* even though he was older than she. To borrow words from Jeremiah, she had not gone running after some poor but handsome man of her own age, like "a wild ass . . . in her heat sniffing the wind," saying "It is hopeless, for I have loved strangers, and after them I will go" (Jer. 2:24-25). Likewise she had not selfishly sought marriage with a "rich" man (a different word from that in Ruth 2:1) unrelated to Naomi's extended family *(mishpahah)*. She acted in accordance with the wisdom of Proverbs: "Riches do not profit in the day of wrath, but righteousness delivers from death" (Prov. 11:4).

A woman of worth (3:11 RSV). Second, Boaz showed his respect for Ruth by calling her "a woman of worth." Further, he assured her that he would honor her request by marrying her and acting as next-of-kin to rescue Naomi and the family of Elimelech from extinction. Thus, at the end of the harvest season, Ruth — who appeared in Boaz's field as a strange woman *(nokriya)* from Moab among a people she did not know (2:11), who asked only to be a female servant *(shiphhah,* 2:13) — was now known by everyone in town as "a woman of worth," that is, possessing *hayil.*

As stated in 2:1, Boaz was "a man of substance" or *hayil* (NJPS). This referred not only to Boaz's wealth but also to his moral stature (see above, 24-25). For Ruth, *hayil* referred to her loyalty to her mother-in-law, her hard work in the harvest field, and her virtue, rather than to the female ability to "produce children," as the term *hayil* has been translated in 4:11.

Other translations of the Hebrew expression "a woman of *hayil*" are possible: "a virtuous woman" (KJV), "a fine woman" (REB, TEV, NJPS), "a woman of noble character" (NIV), "a capable woman" (NEB). These all express the opposite of the "loose woman" *(zarah),* used in parallel with *nokriya,* "adulteress" (Prov. 2:16; 7:5; cf. 5:20). The Hebrew ideal woman was "a capable wife (a wife possessing *hayil)* . . . far more precious than jewels" (Prov. 31:10). She would be a skillful gardener and seamstress, providing food and clothing for her household. As a businesswoman she would purchase land, plant a vineyard, and make a profit from her transactions. She would embody the Israelite ideal of benevolence by helping the poor and needy. She would be a wise teacher of her children, a model of "strength and dignity," with reverence for the LORD (from Prov. 31:11-31).

"Do not be afraid" (3:11). Third, Boaz reassured Ruth that she had nothing to fear. Readers may speculate about the meaning of his words, "do not be afraid." Would she be afraid of his physical strength to overpower her at midnight? The reader would

think of how Amnon "forced" his half sister Tamar and "lay with her" (2 Sam. 13:14). Might Boaz decide to make this foreign woman his maidservant or concubine? She had put herself into his power. He could accept or reject her request for marriage, could ruin her, exploit her for his own selfish purpose, or act with covenant loyalty toward her.

Boaz reassured her with his twice-repeated word "and now" (Ruth 3:11, 12), matching Naomi's call to action (v. 2). He assured Ruth that the moment had come for *him* to take action on her behalf.

"Another kinsman" (3:12). Fourth, Boaz told Ruth that there was a kinsman closer than he who had the duty to act as next-of-kin, that is, to rescue the family of Elimelech from extinction. Boaz could not act on his promise to marry Ruth until this legal matter was settled. Yet his vow, "As the LORD lives, I will act as next-of-kin for you" (3:13), reveals both his eager personal response to Ruth's initiative and his willingness to act out his covenant loyalty toward the "[extended] family of Elimelech" (2:1).

"As the LORD *lives"* (3:13). Fifth, Boaz's oath using the expression "as the LORD lives" bound his spoken words to the power and grace of the living God. This kind of oath was often accompanied by evidence that the LORD was indeed "living" and active. For example, someone could take an oath by the living God "who saves Israel" (1 Sam. 14:39), "who has saved my life from every adversity" (1 Kgs. 1:29), "who gave us our lives" (Jer. 38:16), or "who brought the people of Israel up out of the land of Egypt" (Jer. 16:14).

We may imagine a similar statement by Boaz: "As the LORD lives who has given us a good crop after years of famine . . ." (cf. Ruth 1:6), or ". . . whose kindness has not forsaken the living or the dead" (2:20), or who has "remembered his covenant, and showed compassion according to the abundance of his steadfast love" (Ps. 106:45). The person taking such an oath would be empowered by the living LORD to act according to the words spoken.

Once again (see above, 35), we see Boaz as a model of the covenant manner of life in Israel, which was to "fear . . . worship

. . . and [swear] by his name alone" (Deut. 10:20; cf. 6:13). From the perspective of Jeremiah, when Boaz swore " 'As the LORD lives!' in truth, in justice, and in uprightness" (Jer. 4:2), he was contributing to the health and integrity of the society of Bethlehem, Judah, and all Israel. Boaz's oath would be a rebuke to a sick society where people "say, 'As the LORD lives,' yet they swear falsely" (Jer. 5:2). Hosea told his people not to "enter into Gilgal, or go up to Beth-aven, [or] swear 'As the LORD lives'" (Hos. 4:15). Amos also lived in a time of disintegration and corruption when people would "swear by Ashimah of Samaria, and say 'As your god lives, O Dan,' and 'As the way of Beer-sheba lives'" (Amos 8:14).

Boaz's simple oath was a call to the renewal of integrity in private and public life. Jeremiah saw that restored integrity among God's people would bear fruit not only in Israel, but among the nations who "shall be blessed by him [the LORD], and by him they shall boast" (Jer. 4:2). Deutero-Isaiah looked forward to the time when "every tongue shall swear" in the name of Yahweh (Isa. 45:23) and receive "righteousness and strength" from him (v. 24).

"Lie down until the morning" (3:13). Sixth, Boaz showed his consideration for Ruth by counselling her to remain where she was "until the morning." The night hours must have held many thoughts and feelings of anticipation for both Ruth and Boaz. But the darkness before dawn was time for her to leave the scene. Naomi's instructions to Ruth were that she not make herself known to "the man" until the right time (Ruth 3:3). When, at the right time, she did make herself known to Boaz, there remained the problem of preserving Ruth's honor. Boaz showed his covenant loyalty by seeking to protect her person and name from the danger of going through the streets in the night. Concealed from the public eye by the heap of grain, and protected by his good character, she could "remain this night" without fear. In the dawn's half-light, without making herself known to the public (i.e., before anyone could recognize her), she arose and made her exit (v. 14). With the words "he said" the Narrator makes it clear that this was Boaz's thoughtful precaution lest she compromise her reputation as "a woman of worth" by her daring visit to the threshing floor.

Six Measures of Barley (3:14-15)

Finally, "before one person could recognize another," Boaz poured out six measures of threshed barley for Ruth to take to her mother-in-law. Readers will ask about the significance of the number "six" in this narrative. Here are some suggestions:

1) "Six measures" was probably somewhere between 20 and 40 kg. (or from 50 to 85 lbs.) and was about double the amount of grain in the ephah that Ruth had gathered in a day of gleaning (2:17; see above, 35). It was a mark of Boaz's generosity, and of Ruth's robust strength as she carried it home.

2) The Narrator used the number six as a recollection of the sixth day of creation on which God created men and women in his image (Gen. 1:27).

3) The number six indicates partial fulfillment of Yahweh's "reward" and anticipates the seventh measure, the "full reward" (Ruth 2:12).

MORNING LIGHT (3:16-18)

Naomi: "Who Are You?" (3:16)

Naomi, waiting with anticipation at home, greeted Ruth in the morning light with a strange question, literally, "Who are you, my daughter?" All modern English versions of the Bible translate Naomi's question with words similar to those of the NRSV: "How did things go with you, my daughter?" (3:16). This is, however, a paraphrase of the Hebrew that is preserved in the KJV. Perhaps the original makes more sense if we paraphrase it in the following way: "Who is this carrying such a huge load of grain with a big smile on your face? What change is this that has come over you? Are you still my loyal Moabite daughter-in-law gleaning in the fields for food?"

Boaz's two questions about Ruth's identity ("To whom does this woman belong?" [2:5] and "Who are you?" [3:9]) each signified a change in her relationship to him. Now Naomi's question likewise marks a new stage in Ruth's relationship to Naomi. Her daughter-in-law was about to become Boaz's wife. Would she forget her pledge of loyalty made to Naomi back in Moab?

50

Fullness for Emptiness (3:17)

Ruth reassured Naomi by stating the meaning of the gift of six measures of barley: Boaz did not want Ruth to return to Naomi "empty-handed" (Heb. *reqam*). This word recalls Naomi's bitterness when she arrived back in Bethlehem:

> I went away full,
>   but the LORD has brought me back empty. (*reqam*, 1:21)

The six measures of threshed grain were a partial filling of the emptiness. Yahweh's kindness (*hesed*) was becoming a reality through Ruth's loyalty to her family, the daring initiative of Naomi and Ruth, and the generous response of Boaz. Boaz was applying the injunction concerning the liberation of slaves to a widow trapped in poverty: "You shall not send him [her] out empty-handed. Provide liberally out of . . . your threshing floor" (Deut. 15:13-14).

How It Will Turn Out (3:18)

Naomi's last words in the story instruct Ruth to "wait" (lit., "sit still") quietly while Boaz (here identified simply as "the man") responded actively to the midnight encounter between "the man" and the "woman" (3:8) at the threshing floor.

At the end of the period of waiting Ruth would "learn how the matter turns out" (3:18). The future, even the day that lay ahead, was full of mystery, with many possibilities, seemingly dependent on chance, luck, or fate. When Ruth went out to glean, she "happened" to arrive at Boaz's field (2:3). Would the unseen hand of God guide the events of the day that lay ahead?

Note on Female Role Models   The OT describes a limited number of women who were held up as role models. The midwives Shiphrah and Puah refused to obey the pharaoh's order to kill all Hebrew male children because they "feared God" (Exod. 1:17). This act preserved the Hebrew community from extinction. Moses' mother and sister cooperated with an Egyptian princess to save the life of Moses, thus making sure his mission of liberation and law-giving (Exod. 2:5-9). Miriam led the escaped slaves in a song of victory after crossing the sea (Exod. 15:20-21) and was remembered with Moses and Aaron for her heroism (Mic. 6:4). Rahab the Canaanite prostitute, by her bold action in saving the lives of the Israelite scouts, helped open the land of Canaan (Josh. 2:1-21) and preserved her own kindred alive (6:22-23, 25). Deborah was "a mother in Israel" (Judg. 5:7), who empowered her people to win victory on the battlefield against the oppressors.

A wise woman of Abel Beth-maacah saved her city from destruction by her "wise plan." Calling herself "one of those who are peaceable and faithful in Israel" (2 Sam. 20:14-22), she negotiated a peace with Joab, David's commander. Huldah the prophetess gave divine approval to the contents of the scroll found in the temple, and set in motion the great reformation of King Josiah (2 Kgs. 22:14-20).

Did some wise female sage inspire the writer of Prov. 1, 8, and 9 to picture the wisdom of God as Lady "Wisdom"? Why did this writer portray wisdom as a gracious woman who "cries out in the street . . . the busiest corner . . . the entrance to the city gates" (Prov. 1:20-21; cf. 8:1-5) with words of wise counsel for the public and private life of all? The writer speaks of her as one who inspires rulers to promote justice (Prov. 8:15-16), and invites the foolish to "come, eat of my bread and drink of the wine I have mixed," to "lay aside immaturity, and live" (9:5, 6).

The Narrator of the story of Ruth stands with a minority of OT writers who challenge the dominant patriarchal culture and emphasize the importance of the initiative, daring, and wisdom of women "of worth" in ancient Israel. These writers point to women's skills in the arts, commerce and business, education, politics, and medicine. They affirm that women share in divine wisdom itself.

From our contemporary world we may compare Ruth's commitment to her mother-in-law, and her willingness to leave her old environment in order to open up the future for Naomi, with the dedication of women pastors to their church.

A Chinese woman pastor's reflections on her dedication to the demands of church life, which involved her in difficult choices between work and family, suggest a comparison with Ruth's dedication to Naomi and her long days of gleaning in the harvest fields of Bethlehem:

> When I offered my life to the church, the whole family, including my husband and child, became a part of that offering. I get up very early in the morning to send my son to the child care center. [A pastor has many unexpected responsibilities, and] I cannot always be on time to pick him up [at the end of the day]. Sometimes I find him waiting, standing alone at the gate of the center like a motherless child. I cannot stop my tears streaming down.

A comment by the one interviewing several women pastors further illustrates the analogy and draws an appropriate lesson:

> Even with such heavy burdens, the women pastors were light-hearted throughout the interview, laughing as they talked. We hope that the whole church, and all members of the body of Christ, can be aware of the situation of their faithful, committed church workers, especially women. We speak daily of the harvest being plentiful and the laborers few. As [these women pastors] bend down in the field all day with their sickles in hand, let us give them a towel to wipe off their sweat, and a cup of cold water to quench their thirst. Building up the household of God depends not only on the pastor, but on all of us as well. Let us be more sensitive to our women pastors, and listen to the voices from their hearts, so that they can serve the church without worries.

Another word from a Chinese pastor's husband reminds us of Boaz's kindness and consideration for Ruth:

> Our family is built on a common faith. After graduation from the university I too had thought about being a church worker. But that never materialized. Therefore I want to do all I can to help my wife in her ministry of theological education. By doing so I also find fulfillment of my own dream. . . . Her

income from the church is low, but all my income is shared for the expenses of our home. . . . I have experienced first hand how much a woman pastor needs the support of her family, especially her husband. . . . While some of the women church workers have problems due to their families' lack of faith commitment, other factors such as the church not giving women their rightful place also need to be dealt with. Still, what a God-loving husband can contribute to help is very obvious. I find my life more valuable and worth living because I am able to help my wife serve God in her work. I too am committed to God, serving in a different manner. May all God-loving spouses of women pastors be able to say from the depths of their hearts: "I am proud of my wife who is a pastor." (These examples come from Jean Woo, "China News Update.")

HOPE FULFILLED

Ruth 4:1-22

The story of Ruth reaches its climax at the Bethlehem city gate in the bright morning light, where the promises made beside the heap of grain the night before must be kept, and where those once hopeless will have their hope fulfilled. In keeping with the patriarchal nature of Israelite society, neither Ruth nor Naomi appears in this scene. Boaz, the ten elders, and "So-and-so" the next-of-kin will make decisions for the women. The name Boaz, mentioned only twice in Ruth 3, appears seven times in 4:1-12. Now it is Boaz's turn to "settle the matter today" (3:18), while Naomi and Ruth wait quietly at home for the unfolding of events that they themselves have initiated.

This chapter tells of the marriage of Ruth and Boaz. Speeches by Boaz (4:9-10), the people at the gate (vv. 11-12), and the women of Bethlehem (vv. 14-15, 17a) give three different views of the marriage, to which the Narrator adds a fourth (vv. 18-22). In the views here expressed we may find clues to the intentions, hopes, and blessings inherent in events at the gate. We may also glimpse dimensions of this marriage that find echoes in the human community, and reveal the redemptive purpose of God that lies behind the joining of two lives together.

WHO WILL BE THE REDEEMER? (4:1-8)

The Next-of-kin? (4:1)

As soon as Boaz sat down on one of the benches at the city gate, the next-of-kin "came passing by" (4:1). As in 2:3, where, "as it happened," Ruth came to glean in the field belonging to Boaz, the reader will sense the Narrator's intention to suggest that divine providence lay behind this seemingly chance happening. The fact that he happened to pass by at that moment made it possible for Boaz to "settle the matter" (3:18) that very day.

The next-of-kin remains nameless. Boaz called him "So-and-so" (NJPS) or "friend" (NRSV), an interpretation of a meaningless Hebrew expression. He is important only as a legal obstacle to the fulfillment of Boaz's promise to Ruth. His words, "I cannot redeem it for myself without damaging my own inheritance" (4:6), cleared the way for Boaz to carry out his plans.

Redemption: A Legal Transaction (4:2)

Witnesses were necessary in order to make the transaction legal. The ten elders who gathered at the gate at Boaz's invitation to "sit down here" were people of standing who maintained and upheld the Bethlehem community (cf. Deut. 27:1; Josh. 24:1). Although there were others who witnessed the decision about to be made ("all the people who were at the gate," Ruth 4:11), it was the elders who made it legal.

The Hebrew word translated "elder" means, literally, "someone with a beard," that is, an adult male. Elders could serve as judges in disputes (Deut. 21:1-9; 22:15-18) or witnesses to administrative decisions (25:5-9). Boaz, as "a prominent rich man" (Ruth 2:1), might well have been an elder himself.

The Right of Redemption

We have already considered the custom of redemption in the discussion of Ruth 2:1 (see above, 25-26). Here once again, the terms "next-of-kin" (*go'el*), "redeem" (*ga'al*), and "right of redemption" (*ge'ullah*) are keys to a proper understanding of this scene at the gate. Ancient Israel's system of social security through family solidarity with the poor and needy is the framework for the action described here. The term "next-of-kin" (*go'el*), echoing Ruth's request and Boaz's promise at the threshing floor (3:13), appears four times (4:1, 3, 6, 8), the term "redeem" (*ga'al*) six times (4:4, 6), and the expression "the right of redemption" *(ge'ullah)* once (4:6). The question was not *whether* there would be anyone to rescue or "redeem" Ruth and Naomi, but rather, *who* had the right and obligation to do so. The next-of-kin was acting according to the law of redemption in Leviticus:

> Throughout the land that you hold, you shall provide for the redemption *(ge'ullah)* of the land. If anyone of your kin falls into difficulty and sells a piece of property, then the next-of-kin *(go'el)* shall come and redeem *(ga'al)* what the relative has sold. (Lev. 25:24-25)

Elimelech had apparently owned a portion or "parcel" of a larger field (Ruth 4:3). When he and his family went to Moab, the piece of land was farmed by others. When Naomi returned, she still had title to, but not the use of the land. She was like the widow in the time of Elisha who left her parcel of land during a time of famine, went to the territory of the Philistines, but later returned to claim her house and land (2 Kgs. 8:1-6). Naomi had apparently decided to sell her piece of land because of her poverty (Ruth 4:3).

At first the next-of-kin said to Boaz, "I will redeem it" (4:4), thinking that he could get the profit from its cultivation, while keeping it in the family. In this way he would be acting honorably according to the law of family solidarity to "maintain the dead man's name on his inheritance" (v. 5).

However, the presence of Naomi's daughter-in-law, the widow of Elimelech's deceased son Mahlon, made this more than a matter of the redemption of land. It meant rescuing the family of Elimelech from extinction by begetting a son from Mahlon's widow. This son would have rights to the parcel of land, so that the next-of-kin would have to return it to the son. This explains the next-of-kin's change of mind, saying "I cannot redeem it for myself without damaging my own inheritance" (v. 6).

The Transfer of the Right of Redemption (4:7-8)

The shoe ceremony at the Bethlehem gate was probably like signing a document of transfer. When the next-of-kin removed his shoe, he was giving up his right of redemption (*ge'ullah*) to the parcel of land. When he gave it to Boaz in the presence of the ten elders and the other people at the gate, he transferred his right of redemption to Boaz.

The Narrator's historical note explains a custom from former times, no longer practiced in the Narrator's time. The purpose of the ceremony was to give legal status to a transfer of responsibility involving "redeeming and exchanging" (4:7).

Note on the Meaning of the Shoe Ceremony   Readers today will want some additional explanation about the meaning of the removal of a shoe, which was the covering of the foot. We must look elsewhere in the OT for clues about the meaning of the foot, or shoe. The foot may symbolize power or possession. The psalmist tells us that God gave humans dominion over all creation, that is, "put all things under their feet" (Ps. 8:6). Another psalmist asked that "the foot of the arrogant" not be allowed to tread on him (Ps. 36:11). When the Israelite army chiefs placed their feet on the necks of the Canaanite kings, this was a symbol of their power over those kings (Josh. 10:24).

The foot also symbolized territorial claims. God promised to give to his people "every place on which you set foot" (Deut. 11:24; cf. Josh. 1:3). Caleb claimed land around Hebron on which he had set foot (Deut. 1:36; Josh. 14:9). Records recovered from the ancient Mesopotamian city of Nuzi attest to a ceremony of transfer of land ownership in which the old owner would lift up his foot and place the new owner's foot on the piece of land (Ernest R. Lacheman, "Note on Ruth 4:7-8").

Removal of shoes could symbolize surrender of power or authority. Moses (Exod. 3:5) and Joshua (Josh. 5:15) removed their shoes to show their own humility before the awesome power of God. When David walked barefoot up the Mount of Olives, he showed his powerlessness in the face of his son's rebellion (2 Sam. 15:30). Isaiah and Micah walked barefoot to show the humiliation of war prisoners (Isa. 20:2-4; Mic. 1:8).

Another shoe ceremony (Deut. 25:5-10; see above, 14) should be mentioned in connection with the ceremony recorded in Ruth 4:7-8. It is related to the "levirate marriage" custom, according to which the husband's brother (Latin *levir*) was required to marry his brother's widow in order to give his deceased brother an heir. If the brother-in-law refuses to do his duty, the widow removes her brother-in-law's shoe as a public humiliation of "the man who does not build up his brother's house" (Deut. 25:9). This law is not relevant to Ruth 4:7-8, however, since there is no sense of wrongdoing by the next-of-kin, and hence no need for public humiliation. Neither the next-of-kin nor Boaz was a brother of Ruth's deceased husband Mahlon.

FOUR VIEWS OF THE MARRIAGE

(1) BOAZ'S VIEW: A FUTURE FOR THIS FAMILY (4:9-10)

Boaz's last speech in the story defines his role in the agreement about to take place. It begins and ends with the words to the ten elders and the people gathered at the gate: "Today you are witnesses" (Ruth 4:9, 10). This refers to the agreement implied in the shoe ceremony. The response of the people, "We are witnesses" (v. 11), confirmed the agreement. Clearly the marriage of Ruth and Boaz was a matter of concern for the whole community, not a private affair between two people.

Kinship Obligations

a) *Land.* Marriage involved kinship obligations. Unlike Samson, who took revenge on the father of his Philistine bride by setting fire to his grainfields and orchards (Judg. 15:4), Boaz accepted the responsibility of relieving the burden of Naomi's poverty by "acquiring" (Heb. *qanah*) from the hand of Naomi "all that belonged to Elimelech and . . . Chilion and Mahlon" (Ruth 4:9). This involved the purchase of Elimelech's parcel of land now held by Naomi.

By acquiring this piece of land in an act of family solidarity, Boaz was beginning to restore the fortunes of Naomi from the poverty of widowhood, and Elimelech's family from being cut off. The best parallel to Boaz's purchase of Naomi's land as an act of redemption is the action of Jeremiah when Jerusalem was under siege from the Babylonian armies. His cousin Hanamel asked him to "buy" *(qanah)* a field because "the right of redemption *(ge'ullah)* by purchase *(qanah)*" belonged to Jeremiah (Jer. 32:7). Two copies of "the sealed deed of purchase, containing the terms and conditions" (v. 11) were hidden in an earthenware jar (v. 14). The purpose of this action was to show Jeremiah's faith that in the future "fields and vineyards shall again be bought *(qanah)* in this land" (v. 15), and "deeds shall be signed and sealed and witnessed . . . in the places around Jerusalem, and in the cities of Judah . . ." (v. 44). In the time to come, Jeremiah believed, Yahweh would "restore their fortunes" (32:44). Similarly, Boaz's purchase of Elimelech's piece of land from Naomi, thus keeping it in the family, was an act of faith that Yahweh would restore the fortunes of Elimelech's family.

b) *Marriage.* The main point of the marriage, however, was not the acquisition of a piece of land. Boaz stated before the witnesses at the gate his full acceptance of "Ruth the Moabite, the wife of Mahlon, to be my wife" (Ruth 4:10). She was not to be his female slave *(shiphhah,* as in 2:13) or his household servant *(amah,* as in 3:9) but his wife. This marriage was the formation of "one flesh" (Gen. 2:24), or "one new humanity in place of the two" (Eph. 2:15).

The reader may be surprised to note that Boaz used the verb "acquire" *(qanah)* in the case of Ruth, just as in the case of the piece of land (Ruth 4:9). Did this verb imply that he had "acquired" Ruth the foreigner as his "property" (see Lev. 25:44-45)? Probably not, since he wanted to make Ruth his "wife," not his property.

When used with persons, the verb *qanah* can mean "recover" in the sense of "rescue," as in the expression "the LORD will recover *(qanah)* the remnant that is left of his people" (Isa. 11:11). The words "acquire" and "redeem" are used in parallel by the psalmist in his prayer:

> Remember your congregation, which you acquired long ago,
>   which you redeemed to be the tribe of your heritage.
>
> (Ps. 74:2)

God's purpose in "acquiring" his people was to "redeem" *(ga'al)* them. By acting as next-of-kin or redeemer (Ruth 3:13) when he made Ruth his wife, Boaz gave a future to the family of her late husband.

The Name of the Dead

As Naomi had praised Yahweh, "whose kindness has not forsaken the living or the dead" (2:20), so Boaz recognized that marriage was a participation in God's plan "in choosing and calling a people whose vitality must be preserved from generation to generation" (see above, 37). Partners bring to marriage their ties to past generations. Ruth's ties were to Mahlon, her late husband who had died in Moab, far away from Bethlehem. Boaz's obligation in marrying her was to "maintain the dead man's name on his inheritance" (4:10). This meant three areas of continuity: the family circle, the public memory, and a secure place for future generations.

In the family circle. With the hope of an heir, the name of Mahlon would not be "blotted out of Israel" (Deut. 25:6). The names of Elimelech and Mahlon would continue as vital links in the succession of generations across the years.

Two individuals illustrate the Israelite fear lest the line of continuity between past and future generations be broken. Saul pleaded with David not to "cut off my descendants after me . . . [nor] wipe out my name from my father's house" (1 Sam. 24:21). Absalom, who had "no son to keep my name in remembrance," erected a monument to himself called "Absalom's Monument" (2 Sam. 18:18).

Continuity with the past has been of great importance in many cultures of Asia. Tablets with the names of ancestors of former generations were part of the Confucian cult. In the past, in some parts of Indonesia, the embalmed corpse of an ancestor was kept seated in an upright position in the home. Tiered towers in Bali temples honor family ancestors. In Thailand, a son who does not perform rites in honor of his dead father is thought to be breaking the continuous line with the past.

In the rapidly changing society of today, readers will ask about the best way to keep the remembrance of former generations alive. They will ask how to honor deceased parents and grandparents.

Maintaining the continuity of generations does not mean perpetuating the errors and wrongs of the past. In the days before the fall of Jerusalem, Jeremiah said that "our ancestors have inherited nothing but lies." In addition, they had forgotten Yahweh's name for Baal. Jeremiah warned that the guilt of parents would have bad effects on their children. In fact, children were complaining that they had suffered from the sins of their parents (Jer. 16:19; 23:27; 31:29). The prophet Zechariah spoke clearly: "Do not be like your ancestors" (Zech. 1:4).

The best way to honor past generations is rather to maintain continuity of faith in the God of the ancestors.

> In you our ancestors trusted;
> > they trusted, and you delivered them.
> To you they cried, and were saved;
> > in you they trusted, and were not put to shame.
>
> (Ps. 22:4-5)

In the public memory. A second kind of continuity in ancient Israel is symbolized by the word "gate" (Ruth 4:10). According to Israelite custom, the son to be born to Boaz and "Ruth the . . . wife of Mahlon" would be considered an heir of Mahlon. This heir would keep alive the memory of his father's and grandfather's name by virtuous deeds of covenant loyalty and wisdom in the public assembly.

The "gate" was the location of public assemblies, where agreements were witnessed (4:1) and justice done, or left undone (Amos 5:15). People would gather around the public well at the city gate (2 Sam. 23:15) and praise the good works of virtuous men and women (Prov. 31:23, 31; cf. Ruth 3:11, where the Hebrew word for "gate" is translated "assembly"). They would seek or reject wisdom at "the entrance of the city gates" (Prov. 1:21).

A place for descendants. A third kind of continuity is symbolized by the word "native place" (Ruth 4:10), which, in Hebrew, is separate from "gate." Through his heir, Mahlon would continue to have a legitimate place or home in the society of Bethlehem.

Elimelech and his family left their home when they went from Judah to Moab (1:1). Naomi set out from Moab, the temporary "place where she had been living," to return to "the land of Judah" where her family had a place (1:7). Boaz saw his marriage with Ruth as a way of preserving the "native place" *(maqom)* of the heirs of Mahlon and Elimelech (cf. 2 Sam. 21:5). To use a figure of speech, there would always be a "place" for their descendants at the family table.

Note on "Place" The Hebrew word *maqom* is derived from the verb "to stand," and thus means a place to stand with security "upon a rock" (Exod. 33:21; cf. 3:5). "Place" (Heb. *maqom*) is where a family, tribe, or people can live with security across the generations. For the people of Israel it was the land that Yahweh "prepared" for his people (Exod. 23:20), where "they may live in their own place, and be disturbed no more" (2 Sam. 7:10). It was the "place of [their] ancestors' graves" (Neh. 2:3). The word may refer to the traditional territory of a tribe (Judg. 19:16), or a family "home" (*maqom*, Judg. 7:7; 1 Sam. 2:20). The fear of some Israelites who had been forced to live in other lands was that there would be no "place" for them in Israel when they returned: "In time to come your children might say to our children, 'What have you to do with the LORD, the God of Israel? . . . you have no portion in the LORD'" (Josh. 22:24, 25).

Death was the disrupter of continuity. After death, a person's "place" would not "know" (– remember, Ps. 103:16) or "behold them" (i.e., the dead) any more (Job 20:9). The death of Elimelech and his sons in Moab brought the threat that their "place" would forget them completely, and that they would "have no place in all the territory of Israel" (2 Sam. 21:5). The boldness of Naomi and Ruth, combined with the generous response of Boaz, meant that their "native place" or home would continue to "know" and honor Elimelech and Mahlon long after their death.

Some in Israel knew that there was no security except with Yahweh their true "dwelling place in all generations" (Ps. 90:1;

cf. 91:9, using a different Hebrew word). Jesus, who had "nowhere to lay his head," called on his followers to be ready for this kind of life (Matt. 8:20). In the Gospel of John, he promised to "prepare a place" for them (John 14:2, 3). NT writers saw Abraham as their example. He "set out for a place that he was to receive as an inheritance . . . [looking] forward to the city that has foundations, whose architect and builder is God." They saw their ancestors as "strangers and foreigners on the earth . . . seeking a homeland . . . that is, a heavenly one" (Heb. 11:8, 10, 13, 14, 16). In the meantime, the people of God should "enlarge the site *(maqom)*" of their dwelling (Isa. 54:2) in order to welcome returning sons and daughters looking for their own place at the family table in a "day of salvation" (49:8).

(2) THE PEOPLE'S VIEW: A FUTURE FOR THE PEOPLE OF GOD (4:11b-12)

The people at the gate gave the newly married pair three wishes, each of which emphasized the role of the new family in strengthening the whole people of God.

The House of Israel

The first wedding wish was that Ruth, on coming into the "house" of Boaz, be enabled by Yahweh to "build up" "the house of Israel." The term "house of Israel" is an idiom meaning the whole people of Israel (cf. Exod. 40:38; Num. 20:29). Christians will compare this term with the Church as the people of God. "The whole house of Israel" should, in the words of Jeremiah, be "a name, a praise, and a glory" for Yahweh (Jer. 13:11) among the nations. The function of the "house" of Boaz and Ruth was to "build up" the house of Israel and so bring honor and fame for Yahweh to that part of Israel which was in Bethlehem in Judah.

The people's wish was that Ruth would emulate the two ancestral women, Rachel and Leah. Yahweh gave each power to conceive children (Gen. 29:31; 30:22). Ruth had been married for a number of years without children, and could be considered barren. The effect of the blessing was that the children of Ruth and Boaz would "build up" the whole people of God. This implies a good family environment for the children, so that they would keep the commands of Yahweh. They would then be "like saplings, well-tended in their youth; . . . [their] daughters . . . like cornerstones trimmed to give shape to a palace" (Ps. 144:12 NJPS). We can imagine Ruth saying to them:

> My child, do not forget my teaching,
>   but let your heart keep my commandments;
> for length of days and years of life
>   and abundant welfare they will give you.
> Do not let loyalty *(hesed)* and faithfulness forsake you;
>   bind them around your neck,
>   write them on the tablet of your heart.
> So you will find favor and good repute
>   in the sight of God and of people.
>
>   (Prov. 3:1-4)

The importance of the family of Ruth and Boaz is underlined for later generations by Jeremiah's prophetic word that the "house of Israel" had, in his time, been faithless to Yahweh (Jer. 3:20), and, as a result, would be uprooted and broken down. Jeremiah also said that Yahweh would "build and plant" the nation once again (Jer. 31:28) through new families in the future. Yahweh would "cause a righteous Branch to spring up for David" (i.e., a descendant of Ruth and Boaz). This Davidic king would "execute justice and righteousness in the land" (Jer. 33:15).

A Family of Worth

The second wedding wish was in two parts. Part one was a wish that Boaz, with Ruth by his side, would "prosper in Ephrathah" (Ruth 4:11 RSV). The word "prosper" is a translation of a Hebrew expression that includes the word *hayil*. Readers will recall that Boaz was a man of "worth" (possessing *hayil*, 2:1), and Ruth was a woman of "worth" (possessing *hayil*, 3:11). Together, this man of "worth" and woman of "worth" would become a family of "worth." In other words, they would "prosper." By looking at other verses where this word occurs, we find that their "worth" could include "wealth" (Deut. 8:18), "cattle . . . flocks and . . . goods" (Num. 31:9; *hayil* is translated as "booty"), as well as "gold, silver, and garments" (Zech. 14:14). "Worth" could also include strength to "do valiantly" (i.e., act with *hayil*) against the forces of evil and death (Ps. 60:12). Like the "capable wife" (woman of *hayil*) of Prov. 31:10, a family of worth would have strength to do good works in their community. Such a family would "go from strength *(hayil)* to strength" (Ps. 84:7) as their spiritual vigor increased with the help of God (see Hermann Eising, "*ḥayil*," 354).

Note on Translation   Ruth 4:11 is the only example where it is possible to interpret the phrase here translated "prosper" to mean "produce children" (solely in NRSV) by tying its meaning to v. 10. The problem with this interpretation is that the verb is in the second person masculine singular imperative form, and must refer to Boaz. Children, "a heritage from the LORD" (Ps. 127:3), would be included as part, but not all, of the meaning of "worth" or "strength."

The other part of the second wedding wish was that this family would make Ephrathah (i.e., Bethlehem) famous. The Narrator had already identified Elimelech and his family as "Ephrathites from Bethlehem in Judah" (Ruth 1:2). Readers of the book of Ruth in later years would understand that this wish had been fulfilled in the coming of David, the "son of an Ephrathite of Bethlehem in Judah" (1 Sam. 17:12).

The Lineage of David (4:12)

The third wedding wish compared "this young woman" with Tamar the Canaanite daughter-in-law of Judah, who by her determination to continue the family line, used shocking, even immoral behavior (Gen. 38:13-19). Judah later acknowledged that Tamar was "more righteous" than he himself (Gen. 38:26 RSV). Like Tamar, Ruth had used bold, even provocative behavior, risking the charge of immorality, in order to initiate the process that led to marriage. In a speech similar to Judah's, Boaz acknowledged that "all the assembly of my people know that you are a worthy woman" (Ruth 3:11). In linking the marriage of Ruth and Boaz with "Perez, whom Tamar bore to Judah," the people expressed the wish that the line that began with Tamar and Judah would continue through this family. As the genealogy and the end of the story indicate, this wish was fulfilled in the birth of David.

THE MARRIAGE (4:13)

The Narrator uses five brief expressions to describe the events that followed the ceremony at the gate. First, Boaz "took" Ruth, suggesting a very simple ritual. We may imagine that he went to Naomi's home to escort her to his own home. Ruth was probably not dressed in anything more than her "best clothes" (3:3). She was too poor to own any jewels normally worn by brides (cf. Isa. 61:10). There is no mention of a veil as in the case of Leah or Rachel (cf. Gen. 29:25), no notes about companions of the groom as in the case of Samson (Judg. 14:11), or attendants of the bride as in a royal wedding (Ps. 45:14). In this simple act, Boaz showed his confidence in, and love for Ruth as a "worthy woman" (Ruth 3:11).

In the present canonical setting of the book of Ruth, Boaz's act of "taking" Ruth in marriage stands in vivid contrast to the similar act of the Levite from Ephraim who "took to himself a concubine from Bethlehem in Judah" (Judg. 19:1), and then gave her over to the men of Gibeah, who raped her to death (19:25-27).

The second expression is equally brief: "she became his wife" (Ruth 4:13). The word "became" suggests a mysterious process by which the lives of the "man" *(ish)* and the "woman" *(ishshah,* 3:8) were joined together in "one flesh" (Gen. 2:24), so that each could say, "My beloved is mine, and I am his [or hers]" (Cant. 2:16). This was not a casual union of convenience but a joining of lives in which each would be helper and partner to the other (cf. Gen. 2:20).

The third expression speaks of their sexual union: "they came together" (Ruth 4:13), suggesting a mutuality of sexual relations. In view of the character of both Boaz and Ruth, this translation in the NRSV is more appropriate than the literal translation of the Hebrew, which reads "he went in to her" (RSV). The Hebrew phrase probably means to enter the woman's tent or her chamber. In other circumstances it may describe sexual union with concubines (2 Sam. 16:21) or the wife of another (2 Sam. 12:24; Prov. 6:29), or as family obligation (Gen. 38:8-9).

The fourth expression is a faith statement by the Narrator: "the LORD made her conceive." This is not a simple statement about the union of sperm and egg to create a fetus. The natural process of human reproduction as a gift of God is implied in the words "male and female" and the divine command "be fruitful and multiply," which are part of the creation faith found in Genesis (Gen. 1:27-28). Humans stand in awe at the process by which "breath comes to the bones in the mother's womb" (Eccl. 11:5), when an individual is "knit together" in the womb and "intricately woven in the depths of the earth" (Ps. 139:13, 15).

Ruth's conception was of a special kind, like that of Sarah (Gen. 21:1-2), Rebekah (25:21), Leah (29:31), Rachel (30:22), and the mother of Samson (Judg. 13:3). Like those women, Ruth had been barren. Like them Ruth was, without knowing it, a part of Yahweh's providential plan that began with Abraham, to bring blessing to "all the families of the earth" (Gen. 12:3). The statements about miraculous conception in Genesis assume a perspective long after the event. The writers are giving their interpretation of Yahweh's providential intervention in times long past. Likewise, the Narrator of the story of Ruth made this confident statement of faith about Yahweh's intervention to make Ruth conceive, from a perspective after the death of David (Ruth 4:17).

The final phrase brings the story of Ruth to its climax: "she bore a son." Because of Yahweh's direct intervention, the child of Ruth and Boaz was in a special way a gift from Yahweh. The son would be the one to "maintain the dead man's name on his inheritance" (4:10), to provide security for Naomi (v. 14), and to give Ruth and Boaz a place in the history of God's people (v. 17; cf. Matt. 1:5).

(3) THE WOMEN'S VIEW: A FUTURE FOR NAOMI
(4:14-17)

This is the first time that the women of Bethlehem appear after their greeting of shock and surprise on the return of Naomi from Moab (Ruth 1:19). Here at the end of the story, they turn our attention to Naomi once again with a beautiful blessing on the once bitter woman who was now a joyous grandmother. The blessing tells how Ruth's son, and then Ruth herself, would bring fullness to Naomi who once called her life empty (1:21).

The Grandson's Blessing (4:14-15)

The women spoke of the newborn child as a gift to Naomi from Yahweh who would, in future years, bring three benefits to her.

Protector. As her "next-of-kin" with the right and duty to redeem, the child would protect Naomi, the childless widow, from poverty or other kinds of difficulty (4:14).

Restorer. Second, the grandson would be "a restorer of life." The Hebrew expression occurs seven times in the OT, with varying translations. The effect of food on the starving is to "revive their strength" (Lam. 1:11, 19). The effect of a comforter is to "revive . . . courage" (Lam. 1:16). The work of a defender is to "rescue . . . life" from enemy attacks (Ps. 35:17). For those in danger of death, God will "bring back their souls from the Pit, so that they may see the light of life" (Job 33:30). The divine shepherd "restores my soul" or "my life" (Ps. 23:3 NRSV mg.). Yahweh's covenant teaching (Torah), as lived and taught by this grandson, would mean "reviving the soul" of Naomi (Ps. 19:7), restoring her courage, and strength for life. In him, Naomi would find the answer to the prayer of the poor and needy:

> I am severely afflicted;
>> give me life, O Lord, according to your word."
>>> (Ps. 119:107)

Nourisher. Finally, the newborn child would become for Naomi "a nourisher of your old age" (Ruth 4:15). The women of

Bethlehem described Naomi's old age by a word that means to be gray or have gray hair. Although old age was considered as a time of respect, honor, and beauty (Lev. 19:32; Prov. 16:31; 20:29), it was also seen as a period of life marked by declining strength (1 Kgs. 1:1), failing eyesight (Gen. 27:1; 48:10), disease (1 Kgs. 15:23), and exploitation (Isa. 47:6). In short, old age meant "days of trouble" (Eccl. 12:1). It signified a period of life, especially in the life of a widow, when there is need for a "nourisher."

The word "nourish" may mean to provide food, as in the case of Solomon's officials (1 Kgs. 4:7). The verb is used to describe God's provision of food for Elijah by means of the ravens or the widow (1 Kgs. 17:4, 9), and God's sustaining support of his people during the wilderness years (Neh. 9:21). It could include providing living accommodations as in the case of Joseph's offer to his brothers (Gen. 45:11; 47:12) or David's offer to the aged Barzillai (2 Sam. 19:33).

When a psalmist prayed, "Even to old age and gray hairs, O God, do not forsake me" (Ps. 71:18), or when Deutero-Isaiah spoke God's words to the aging exiles, "Even when you turn gray I will carry you" (Isa. 46:4), they must have been thinking of human "nourishers" or "providers" who would carry out his will. When Zechariah spoke of the future days when "old men and old women shall again sit in the streets of Jerusalem, each with staff in hand because of their great age" (Zech. 8:4), the implication is that God's human agents would cooperate with him to create a peaceful and compassionate society that would nourish the older citizens.

As nourisher of Naomi's old age, her grandson would be obedient to the instruction, "Do not despise your mother when she is old" (Prov. 23:22). With this child near, Naomi could follow the instructions of the psalmist: "Cast your burden on the LORD, and he will sustain [or 'nourish'] you" (Ps. 55:22). Ruth's son would be God's nourishing hands in her old age, and be a sign of the coming salvation for "the remnant of this people" (Zech. 8:6).

A further meaning of the word "nourish" is found in Ruth 4:16. The Narrator has balanced the opening words of vv. 13 and

16 in a way to suggest that the homes of Boaz and Naomi were not far apart. As Boaz "took" Ruth from Naomi's home to be his wife, so now Naomi "took" the child and laid him on her bosom, as his nurse. The Hebrew word translated "nurse" is used of those who are entrusted with the care of, or who take it upon themselves to care for, dependent children or older people. The term "nurse" thus balances the word "nourisher," suggesting that Naomi's care for the child in his years of dependency would lead to her own security in years to come.

The role of Naomi's grandson as "nourisher" will remind readers of the many care-givers, both professional and volunteer, whose love and kindness help older adults in their time of infirmity.

A Daughter-in-law's Blessing (4:15)

Love. The women reminded the once bitter Naomi that Ruth was Yahweh's way of rescuing her from calamity, and that she was still "your daughter-in-law who loves you." This was the women's answer to Naomi's anxious question to Ruth, "Who are you, my daughter?" (Ruth 3:16).

The Hebrew word *ahab* is used to describe the love between Isaac and Rebekah (Gen. 24:67; cf. 29:18), Samson and Delilah (Judg. 16:4; cf. 2 Sam. 13:1), Solomon and his "many foreign women" (1 Kgs. 11:1). It also refers to love between Jacob and his favorite son Joseph (Gen. 37:3), a teacher and disciple (Prov. 9:8), a slave and his master (Exod. 21:5). Only here in the OT, however, does this word describe the love of one woman for another. Love "expresses a genuine deep-rooted bond" that "equates concern for the well-being of one's neighbor with the assertion of one's own will" (Gerhard Wallis, "'āhab," 111). Human love is rooted in God who "loves the strangers" and commands his people to "love the stranger" (Deut. 10:18, 19) and to "love your neighbor as yourself; [because] I am the LORD" (Lev. 19:18).

Ruth had demonstrated her love for Naomi by leaving her "father and mother" and her "native land," and coming "to a people that you did not know before" (Ruth 2:11), as well as her determination to rescue Naomi from poverty through her marriage to Boaz.

71

Total support. The women further reminded Naomi that Ruth was "more to you than seven sons" (4:15). The number "seven" signifies totality or completeness. For Naomi as a woman "too old" (1:12) for any hope of replacing her dead sons by others, Ruth took the place of her sons in helping solve her problems. Perhaps the Narrator thought of Naomi, bereaved and barren but blessed by her daughter-in-law, in terms of Hannah's song in which "The barren has borne seven" (1 Sam. 2:5).

A Name for the Child (4:16-17)

The reader expects Ruth to name her child as did Hannah (1 Sam. 1:20). Alternatively, Boaz, as father, might have named him as did Moses (Exod. 2:22) or David (2 Sam. 12:24). Surprisingly, however, and unique in the Bible, not the parents but the women of Bethlehem gave the newborn boy a name. This suggests that the birth of this child was an event that concerned all the citizens of Bethlehem, as well as the people of Judah and the entire nation.

The name Obed means literally "one who serves," or "one who worships." The name Obed-edom (2 Sam. 6:10) means "one who serves" a deity identified as "Edom." On this analogy, Obed could be a shortened form of *Obed-yahweh*, "one who serves (or 'worships') Yahweh." With a slight change in vowels, *obed* becomes *ebed*, meaning "servant."

The name chosen by the women of Bethlehem was similar to the title given in later years to Yahweh's "servant David," who was destined to save his people (2 Sam. 3:18). David is called Yahweh's "servant" more than 30 times in the OT, and once in the NT (Luke 1:69). Obed (servant of Yahweh) "became the father of Jesse, the father of David" (servant of Yahweh; Ruth 4:17).

As the grandfather of David, Obed would bring honor to Bethlehem (4:11), "be renowned in Israel" (v. 14), and con- tribute to the building up of "the house of Israel" (v. 11). Another Narrator reminds us that Obed was the ancestor of "Joseph the husband of Mary, of whom Jesus was born, who is called the Messiah" (Matt. 1:5, 16; cf. Luke 3:32).

The role of the women of Bethlehem in naming Ruth's son

calls our attention to a second level of meaning to the words that Yahweh "had considered" (or "visited") his people (Ruth 1:6). At the beginning of the story, Yahweh had "visited" his people with a good harvest. At the end of the story Yahweh "visited" his people with a son. The words of Isaiah might well have been on the women's lips:

> For a child has been born for us,
>   a son given to us.
>
> (Isa. 9:6)

(4) THE NARRATOR'S VIEW: A FUTURE FOR SOCIETY (4:18-22)

The brief concluding section of the book of Ruth is a list of ten generations from Perez to David. Like other genealogies, this one shows the continuity of God's purpose. There are two ten-generation lists in Genesis. The first, beginning with Adam, comes to a climax with Noah, whose name means "rest," "serenity," or "comfort" (Gen. 5:1-29). Noah represents a new beginning after the first humans were driven out of the garden of Eden (Gen. 3:24). The second list from Shem to Abraham (Gen. 11:10-26) follows the fall of the Tower of Babel and ends with Abraham, again a sign of new hope for the scattered nations.

The Narrator of the story of Ruth may have had a similar theological purpose in adding this ten-generation genealogy, which comes to a climax with the first mention of David in the Old Testament. In the chaotic period of the judges, when "there was no king in Israel; all the people did what was right in their own eyes" (Judg. 21:25), there was need for someone to bring order out of chaos. In the time of the Narrator, the name of David, like that of Noah and Abraham, would have signified the fulfillment of hope for a new era of peace and stability.

In the dark days after the fall of Jerusalem and the end of the Monarchy, the hoped-for Messiah was seen as a descendant of Ruth's great-grandson David (cf. Ezek. 34:23-24). The writer of the Gospel of Matthew includes the same ten generations from the book of Ruth in a longer genealogy, noting the role of Tamar,

73

Rahab, and Ruth among the ancestors of Jesus the Messiah (Matt. 1:2-6). The words of Zechariah add further depth to the words of the women of Bethlehem in naming Ruth's son:

> Blessed be the Lord GOD of Israel,
>   for he has looked favorably on his people and redeemed them.
> He has raised up a mighty savior for us
>   in the house of his servant David.
>
> (Luke 1:68-69)

As noted, the book of Ruth comes to its end with the first mention of David in the OT: "It is difficult," says Brevard S. Childs, "to overestimate the importance for the biblical tradition of David, who rivals Moses in significance for the entire canon" (*Biblical Theology of the Old and New Testaments*, 153-54).

These last words of the book of Ruth inform the readers of what none of the people in the story — Ruth, Naomi, or Boaz — could have known: the going out from and return to Bethlehem, the bitterness of death and joy in the harvest, the bold initiative and patient waiting, the compassion and generosity, and above all the covenant loyalty so beautifully described in the story were all part of Yahweh's preparation, over a period of several hundred years, for the birth of his chosen servant. Can the community of faith doubt that the same hidden purposes are at work among the nations and communities of our troubled world today?

INTERPRETING THE STORY OF
RUTH TODAY

At the end of a commentary on a particular biblical text, it is fitting to reflect on the task of interpretation by which a text comes into meaningful relationship with the lives of today's readers. The four perspectives on the book of Ruth with which this commentary began are all relevant here.

Looking at it *as a piece of literary art,* we have noted: the development of the story line as it moves from Bethlehem to Moab and back to Bethlehem, from emptiness to fullness, and from bitterness to joy; the moments of dramatic encounter in Moab, the grainfields of Bethlehem, on the threshing floor, and at the Bethlehem gate; the speeches of Naomi, Ruth, Boaz, the people at the gate, and the women of Bethlehem; the recurrence of key words like "fields," "glean," "covenant loyalty," "security," and "Bethlehem," all of which are evidence of the literary skill and clues to the intended emphases of the Narrator.

Reading the book of Ruth *as a work set in a particular historical time,* we have gained insight into the structures of family and society, as well as the customs and laws relating to family solidarity and the protection of the poor in ancient Israel. This in turn has prompted us to look at similarities and differences with family and society of our time.

Reading this book *as part of the canon* has reminded us of the wider witness of the entire Bible. We have frequently compared Ruth with Abraham, who responded to God's call to leave home, kindred, and gods in search of a new society. In its setting following the violent ending of the book of Judges, the book of

Ruth is testimony to the possibilities of an alternative society created by the loyalty and initiative of Naomi and Ruth, the faithfulness of Boaz, and the sustaining support of the community of men and women. Set as it is two generations before the birth of David, and many generations before the birth of David's greatest descendant, this book is witness to the continuity of God's purpose across the ages. Ruth in her bold obedience, resourcefulness, and devotion to Naomi and her conception given by God is a parallel figure to Mary the mother of Jesus. The role of Obed as redeemer, restorer of life, and nourisher of old age anticipates the role of Jesus Christ the Savior of all.

The harvest setting of the story of Ruth reminds the community of faith that, in Hebrew thought, God provides all peoples with grain, waters the furrows, blesses the growth, and crowns the year with his bounty (Ps. 65:9-11; cf. 67:2, 4, 6). A Hebrew prayer at harvesttime was that "your way may be known upon earth, your saving power among all nations," and that the nations should "be glad and sing for joy, for you judge the peoples with equity and guide the nations upon earth" (Ps. 67:3,4). This perspective encourages Christians to reach out to fellow earth-dwellers, and with them to celebrate and preserve the bounty of nature and the goodness of life.

As message from God for the community of faith, the book invites readers to bring their own life experiences, culture, and history to the text for enlightenment, encouragement, and warning.

Many readers will testify to what the story shows of God's mysterious presence then and now, making meetings possible, protecting widows, blessing marriage, giving conception to the barren, and working with humans to bring hope out of despair.

Others who have decided to make a new beginning in their lives by leaving their old ways of living and thinking have found in Ruth an example of a person who made a costly decision to cross cultural and religious boundaries in search of a new life with the people of God.

As a model of "hope for the powerless in every generation" (Bruce Birch, *Let Justice Roll Down*, 311), this story speaks to the human condition in every age — women who are, or need to be, self-reliant and resourceful in difficult circumstances; refugees from war or famine; those with material wealth who hear the challenge to share with the poor; people in an age of ethical confusion who are looking for a challenge to show love and loyalty.

This is a world where "in all our societies, women are the poorest of the poor and the most economically marginalized, unfairly burdened by the current global economic crisis" (Aruna Gnanadason, *No Longer a Secret*, 5). It is a world in which "there is increasing documentation of the many ways in which being female is life-threatening, and a woman is unsafe at every stage of life, even before she is born" (Gnanadason, 6, quoting Charlotte Bunch, "Women's Rights as Human Rights"). An Asian woman finds that "in the highly volatile situations of the world where people and especially women suffer from religious and racial conflicts . . . the wisdom of Ruth should continue to guide us and motivate us to work for justice that is inclusive of all people concerned" (Kwok Pui-lan, "The Future of Feminist Theology: An Asian Perspective"). Biblical scholar Phyllis Trible finds that "the aged Naomi and the youthful Ruth . . . risk bold decisions and shocking acts to work out their own salvation in the midst of the alien, the hostile, and the unknown" (*God and the Rhetoric of Sexuality*, 166).

The alternative vision in the story of Ruth serves as a correction to the ethnocentric views revealed in the postexilic community as seen in the books of Ezra and Nehemiah, when many foreign women and their children were forcibly separated from their husbands, and to similar ethnocentric tensions of our own day. The fact that Ruth is a Moabite, and an outsider, will challenge readers to be more accepting of others.

"There are," writes a professional woman and mother from the United States, "many 'Ruths' in our society today — women who are making sacrifices for the betterment of their family and society. I am sure there is a 'Ruth' in every Christian woman" (private communication from Nancy Sherertz). We would want to add that there are many people like Naomi and Boaz in our time as well.

Naomi's initial reluctance to accept Ruth's offer of love and companionship may have been due to her fear that Ruth would be more of a hindrance than a help to her. This will remind some of the reluctance of many congregations to accept women pastors or give them their rightful place in church leadership. Naomi's subsequent joy at the harvest and the women's assurance of restored hope of protection, new life, and nourishing care brought by Ruth correspond to the joyful discovery by many congregations of the blessings brought by women pastors.

And so, as the community of faith reads, hears, reflects on, and remembers the story of Ruth the Moabite, they will be able to affirm the good news that "surely there is a future, and your hope will not be cut off" (Prov. 23:18). They will invite others, whether women or men, in a world torn by violence, deception, and hopelessness, to share the alternative vision of hope undergirded by deeds of covenant loyalty and the hidden but sure hand of the LORD who makes all things new.

SELECTED BIBLIOGRAPHY

Books

Alter, Robert. *The Art of Biblical Narrative* (New York: Basic Books and London: Allen & Unwin, 1981).

———. *The World of Biblical Literature* (New York: Basic Books, 1992).

———, and Frank Kermode. *The Literary Guide to the Bible* (Cambridge, Mass.: Harvard University Press and London: Collins, 1987).

Auld, A. Graeme. *Joshua, Judges, and Ruth*, Daily Study Bible (Philadelphia: Westminster and Edinburgh: Saint Andrew, 1984).

Birch, Bruce. *Let Justice Roll Down* (Louisville: Westminster John Knox, 1991).

Brenner, Athalya. *The Israelite Woman: Social Role and Literary Type in Biblical Narrative* (Sheffield: JSOT Press, 1985).

Bundesen, Lynne. *The Woman's Guide to the Bible* (New York: Crossroad, 1993).

Campbell, Edward F., Jr. *Ruth*, Anchor Bible (Garden City, N.Y.: Doubleday, 1975).

Childs, Brevard S. *Biblical Theology of the Old and New Testaments* (Minneapolis: Fortress, 1992).

Clines, David J. A. *The Theme of the Pentateuch. JSOT Supplement 10* (Sheffield: JSOT Press, 1978).

Cundall, Arthur, and Leon Morris, *Judges and Ruth* (Downers Grove: InterVarsity, 1968).

Darr, Katheryn Pfisterer. *Far More Precious than Jewels* (Louisville: Westminster John Knox, 1991).

Fewell, Danna Nolan, and David M. Gunn. *Compromising Redemption* (Louisville: Westminster John Knox, 1990).

Gnanadason, Aruna. *No Longer a Secret: The Church and Violence against Women* (Geneva: WCC, 1993).

Gray, John. *Joshua, Judges, Ruth*. Rev. ed. New Century Bible Commentary (Grand Rapids: Wm. B. Eerdmans and Basingstoke: Marshall, Morgan and Scott, 1986).

Hals, Ronald M. *The Theology of the Book of Ruth* (Philadelphia: Fortress, 1969).

Hubbard, Robert L., Jr., *The Book of Ruth*. New International Commentary on the Old Testament (Grand Rapids: Wm. B. Eerdmans, 1988).

Knight, George A. F. *Ruth and Jonah*. 2nd ed. Torch Bible Commentaries (London: SCM, 1966).

Mendenhall, George E. *The Tenth Generation* (Baltimore: Johns Hopkins University Press, 1973).

Sakenfeld, Katharine Doob. *Faithfulness in Action* (Philadelphia: Fortress, 1985).

Sasson, Jack M. *Ruth: A New Translation with a Philological Commentary and a Formalistic Folkloristic Interpretation* (Baltimore: Johns Hopkins University Press, 1979).

Trible, Phyllis. *God and the Rhetoric of Sexuality*. Overtures to Biblical Theology 2 (Philadelphia: Fortress, 1978).

de Waard, Jan, and Eugene A. Nida. *A Translator's Handbook on the Book of Ruth* (New York: American Bible Society, 1973).

Articles

Abraham, K. C. "Ecology and Mission," *Praxis* (Hong Kong: SCM, 1992-93), 12-16.

Bertram, Stephen. "Symmetrical Design in the Book of Ruth," *Journal of Biblical Literature* 84 (1965): 165-68.

Brueggemann, Walter. "The Preacher, the Text, and the People," *Theology Today* 47 (1990): 244.

Bunch, Charlotte. "Women's Rights as Human Rights: Toward a Re-Vision of Human Rights," *Gender Violence: A Development and Human Rights Issue* (New Brunswick, N.J.: Rutgers University Center for Women's Global Leadership, 1991).

Burrows, Millar. "The Ancient Oriental Background of Hebrew Levirate Marriage," *Bulletin of the American Schools of Oriental Research* 77 (1940): 2-15.

————. "The Marriage of Boaz and Ruth," *Journal of Biblical Literature* 59 (1940): 445-454.

Campbell, Edward F., Jr. "The Hebrew Short Story: A Study of Ruth," *A Light Unto My Path* Festschrift for Jacob M. Myers, ed. Howard N. Bream, Ralph D. Heim, and Carey A. Moore (Philadelphia: Temple University Press, 1974), 83-101.

Corona, Mary. "Worth," *In God's Image* (Seoul: Asian Women's Resource Centre for Culture and Theology, December 1, 1993), 62-64.

Eising, Hermann. "*ḥayil [chayil]*," *Theological Dictionary of the Old Testament,* ed. G. Johannes Botterweck and Helmer Ringgren, 4 (Grand Rapids: Wm. B. Eerdmans, 1980): 354.

Fewell, Danna Nolan, and David M. Gunn. "'A Son is Born to Naomi!': Literary Allusions and Interpretation in the Book of Ruth," *Journal for the Study of the Old Testament* 40 (1988): 99-108.

Fisch, Harold. "Ruth and the Structure of Covenant History," *Vetus Testamentum* 32 (1982): 425-437.

Gordis, Robert. "Love, Marriage, and Business in the Book of Ruth: A Chapter in Hebrew Customary Law," *A Light Unto My Path.* Festschrift Jacob M. Myers, 246-264.

Kwok Pui-lan. "The Future of Feminist Theology: An Asian Perspective," *Auburn News* (Fall 1992).

Lacheman, Ernest R. "Note on Ruth 4:7-8," *Journal of Biblical Literature* 56 (1937): 53-56.

Levine, Amy-Jill. "Ruth," *The Women's Bible Commentary,* ed. Carol A. Newsome and Sharon Ringe (Louisville: Westminster John Knox and London: SPCK, 1992), 78-84.

Pantupong, Woranut. "Reflections on Seoul — A Year Later," *Reformed World* 41 (1990): 89-90.

Rowley, H. H. "The Marriage of Ruth," *The Servant of the Lord and Other Essays on the Old Testament,* 2nd ed. (Oxford: Blackwell, 1965), 169-194.

Rylaarsdam, J. Coert. "Weeks, Feast of," *Interpreter's Dictionary of the Bible,* ed. George A. Buttrick (Nashville: Abingdon, 1962), 4:827-28.

Seventh Biannual Conference of the SCM of India, Dec. 29, 1992–January 2, 1993 on the theme "Cry for Life — A Faith Response," *Praxis* (Hong Kong: SCM, 1992-93).

Trible, Phyllis, "Ruth, Book of," *Anchor Bible Dictionary,* ed. David Noel Freedman (New York: Doubleday, 1992), 5:842-47.

Wallis, Gerhard. "*'āhab ['āhabh],*" *Theological Dictionary of the Old Testament,* 1, rev. ed. (Grand Rapids: Wm. B. Eerdmans, 1974), 101-117.

Weinfeld, Moshe. "Ruth, Book of," *Encyclopedia Judaica,* ed. Cecil Roth and Geoffrey Wigoder (Jerusalem: Keter and New York: Macmillan, 1971), 14:518-522.

Woo, Jean. Report from *Tien Feng,* China Christian Council, Shanghai, *China News Update* (Presbyterian Church [U.S.A.], May 1994).